IMAGES OF ENGLAND

CROYDON
AND WADDON

IMAGES OF ENGLAND

CROYDON AND WADDON

RAYMOND WHEELER

Frontispiece: A summer scene at the junction of Crown Hill, George Street and North End taken in August 1935. The traffic policeman appears to have an easy time with only three cars to cope with. Note the advertisements for the Croydon Empire in North End and for Yardley's lavender toilet water.

First published in 2008

The History Press
The Mill, Brimscombe Port,
Stroud, Gloucestershire, GL5 2QG
www.thehistorypress.co.uk

Reprinted 2009, 2012

© Raymond Wheeler, 2008

The right of Raymond Wheeler to be identified as the Author of this work has been asserted in accordance with the Copyrights, Designs and Patents Act 1988.

All rights reserved. No part of this book may be reprinted or reproduced or utilised in any form or by any electronic, mechanical or other means, now known or hereafter invented, including photocopying and recording, or in any information storage or retrieval system, without the permission in writing from the Publishers.

British Library Cataloguing in Publication Data.
A catalogue record for this book is available from the British Library.

ISBN 978 0 7524 4301 0

Typesetting and origination by
The History Press
Printed in Great Britain

Contents

	Introduction	7
one	West Croydon	9
two	North End	23
three	George Street, Wellesley Road and Park Lane	39
four	High Street	67
five	Church Street, Old Town and Duppas Hill	87
six	Waddon	105

Acknowledgements

The photographs appearing in this book have come from various sources and collections, including my own. I am grateful to those who have lent them or given permission for their pictures to be reproduced: Chris Bennett (Croydon Archives Service); Croydon Natural History & Scientific Service; John Gent; William Wood (Whitgift School Archives); Jane McCarthy (Croydon High School Archives); and George Hoole (*Croydon Advertiser*) and Jean Cunnell.

The following photographs have come from the collection belonging to the Croydon Local Studies Library: Page 10b, 11a, 13ab, 16b, 19ab, 20b, 21ab, 22, 24ab, 25b, 26b, 27b, 28a, 29a, 30b, 32, 33, 36b, 37a, 38, 40ab, 41ab, 42ab, 43b, 44b, 45ab, 46, 47ab, 48ab, 49b, 50a, 55b, 56a, 57ab, 58ab, 59b, 60, 62b, 63ab, 64ab, 65a, 66ab, 68ab, 69ab, 70ab, 71ab, 72, 73b, 74ab, 75, 76, 77ab, 78ab, 79ab, 80ab, 81ab, 82, 83ab, 84, 85a, 86ab, 88ab, 89a, 91ab, 92ab, 93ab, 94a, 95a, 96ab, 97ab, 98ab, 99b, 100b, 103b, 104, 106ab, 107ab, 109b, 113a, 114, 115ab, 116, 117, 118b, 119b, 120, 121a, 123b, 124, 125ab, 126.

Croydon Archive Service: 28b, 30a, 49a, 51, 73a, 89b, 119a.

Pamlin Prints: 10a, 30a.

My sincere thanks must go to the following people who have inspired, encouraged or contributed in one way or another in the production of this book including: Steve Roud, Chris Bennett, Christine Corner and all the staff at Croydon Local Studies Library for their support and use of facilities; to Gerry Coll for his encouragement; John Gent; Bill Wood; my colleagues at The Open University in London. Finally, I am indebted to my wife, Susan, for undertaking the task of proofreading and for her valued advice and support.

Introduction

A new word has been coined in recent times; one synonymous with the fashion for ripping out town centres and replacing them with skyscrapers. It is known in architectural circles as 'Croydonisation'. Perhaps much of Croydon's past, as illustrated in this book, has been lost, but much also remains and twenty-first century Croydon has its own heritage which must be conserved for the future.

The name 'Croydon' is of Anglo Saxon origin and may mean 'the valley where wild saffron grows'. Other names in the district are reminders of the densely wooded nature of the area. The original settlement grew up just to the north of an important gap through the North Downs and on the waters of the River Wandle. Evidence of human activity from prehistoric times right up to the Roman period have been found within the locality, including Waddon and Park Hill. A Roman road went through Croydon, perhaps on the line of the present High Street, and an important A.D. fifth and sixth century Saxon cemetery existed in the Edridge Road/Park Lane area. The Domesday Book records a church and a mill, and the adjacent manor house, now the Old Palace, contains fragments of Norman work.

The name Waddon is thought to have been derived from wad-dun or 'woad hill'. Woad, the common name for the flower *isatis tinctoria*, would have grown on the chalk hills and been used by ancient Britons who extracted blue dye from the plant to use as paint. When the houses were built at Aldwick Road on Brandy Bottle Hill, west of the pond, traces of Bronze Age and Iron Age Man were found.

Croydon's links with the Archbishops of Canterbury began in the eighth century and grew over the centuries, with the manor house becoming their country retreat. Its clear trout streams, wooded land in the vicinity, a deer park at Park Hill, and location, only a short distance from London and affairs of state, made it attractive. In 1273 a grant was obtained for a market to be held every Wednesday. Two fairs, authorised under the charters of 1314 and 1343, both survived into the nineteenth century. The principal fair, in later years held between 2-4 October, was known as the Walnut Fair, or October Fair. The fair was probably originally held in the marketplace, but by the end of the Middle Ages, it had moved out of the town centre to the Fairfield, on the eastern edge of the town, where it remained until 1866. The Cherry Fair, held in the market area, survived until 1854. Medieval and Tudor monarchs came to stay at Croydon Palace, and Elizabeth I visited many times, with trade flourishing as a result. By the seventeenth century Croydon was the principal town of East Surrey.

Croydon's inns prospered as trade developed. The earliest and best known was The Greyhound, recorded as early as 1493. Others included the Crown, the Green Dragon, the George, King's Arms and White Lion. Many of these became coaching inns providing accommodation for travellers and stabling for horses. By the seventeenth century, some fifty coaches passed through Croydon daily.

Following the death of Archbishop Hutton in 1758 the palace, by now largely deserted and in disrepair, was sold, becoming a bleaching factory, then a laundry, and finally, at the end of the nineteenth century, a school. The town continued to flourish, with a corn market in the town hall, a provisions market in the butter market, and livestock in Butcher Row, the old name for Surrey Street. Besides agriculture, other industries thrived, including brewing, the tanning of hides, milling, quarrying, shoemaking and brick-making.

The population of Croydon had grown to 5,743 by the dawn of the nineteenth century. Within thirty years this had doubled to 12,479. The centre of the town, still separate from London by open country, spread from the narrow High Street to Old Town and from Crown Hill down towards South End. In 1803 the Surrey Iron Railway opened from Wandsworth to Croydon and in 1809 Croydon was served by a canal with its terminal basin at West Croydon. This was superseded by the London & Croydon Railway, which bought steam-powered transport to the town in 1839.

By 1851, the population had increased to 20,343, bringing with it the problems of overcrowding and poor health due to bad sanitation. In 1849, in response to this situation, Croydon had become one of the first towns in the country to acquire a Local Board of Health. Within two years a pumping station, reservoir, sewage disposal works and several miles of pipes and sewers were constructed. The town continued to grow becoming popular as a pleasant residential area for members of the middle classes who could commute to work in the City of London. A horse-tram system was inaugurated in 1879. By this time the 'market' area had become run down and was now known as Croydon's 'red-light district.'

From the 1890s Croydon, now with a population of 101,795, became of age. The Croydon Improvement Act of 1890 enabled the new council powers to sweep away the 'market' area, widen the High Street and build a new town hall befitting a confident town looking towards the twentieth century. People such as Joshua Allder, Charles Hussey, Louis Turtle and John Ollis Pelton, amongst others, established Croydon as a thriving commercial and retail centre. In 1901, a new electric tramway system opened with a line from Norbury to Purley through North End and High Street as well as a line from George Street, via East Croydon Station, to Addiscombe.

The 1920s and 1930s saw a housing boom not only in the east and south of the borough, but around Waddon too, with a new council estate built. Purley Way was created to serve the new Croydon Airport, placing Croydon on the international map. Purley Way became a new industrial zone.

By the 1930s, the town centre was again becoming congested. After the Second World War, the council decided to introduce another major redevelopment scheme. The Croydon Corporation Act, passed in 1956, coupled with the Government's move to encourage businesses to move out of central London, ensured Croydon became the ideal site as a business centre in the 1960s, with an increasing number of office blocks being built, especially in the area between Wellesley Road and East Croydon Station. Taberner House, finished in 1967, became the administrative centre of the enlarged London Borough of Croydon, created in 1965. In the same period Croydon developed as a centre for shopping, with the Whitgift Centre opening in 1969, Fairfield Halls opened in 1962, and a new underpass, flyover, and several multi-storey car parks were also built.

Croydon has continued to flourish in recent years, as the largest office and retail centre in south-east England, outside central London. At the same time, however, it has often been characterised as dull and inhuman. The late 1980s and 1990s have seen further changes. Many of the outdated 1960s office blocks have been replaced. The pedestrianisation of North End in 1989 and the opening of the Clocktower, an important cultural and arts centre in 1994 may give the town a more attractive image in the future. A new urban light rail system, Croydon Tramlink, began operation in May 2000. The town centre is still a place of leisure with numerous bars, clubs and restaurants.

This compilation of photographs illustrates the town centre and the Waddon area since the mid-nineteenth century. It draws upon the photographic collections of Croydon Local Studies Library, other institutions, and individuals who have kindly given permission for their pictures to be reproduced. A number of pictures have been seen before but many have not. I have arranged them in the form of a journey through various parts of Croydon town centre and travelling westwards towards Waddon. Much has gone yet plenty remains, reminding us of times past. This book is for those who want to explore how Croydon town centre came to be. I hope this book gives you great pleasure, acting as a reminder of bygone days, whilst recognising Croydon needs to continue to change and develop if it wishes to retain its vitality and independence.

Ray Wheeler
May 2008

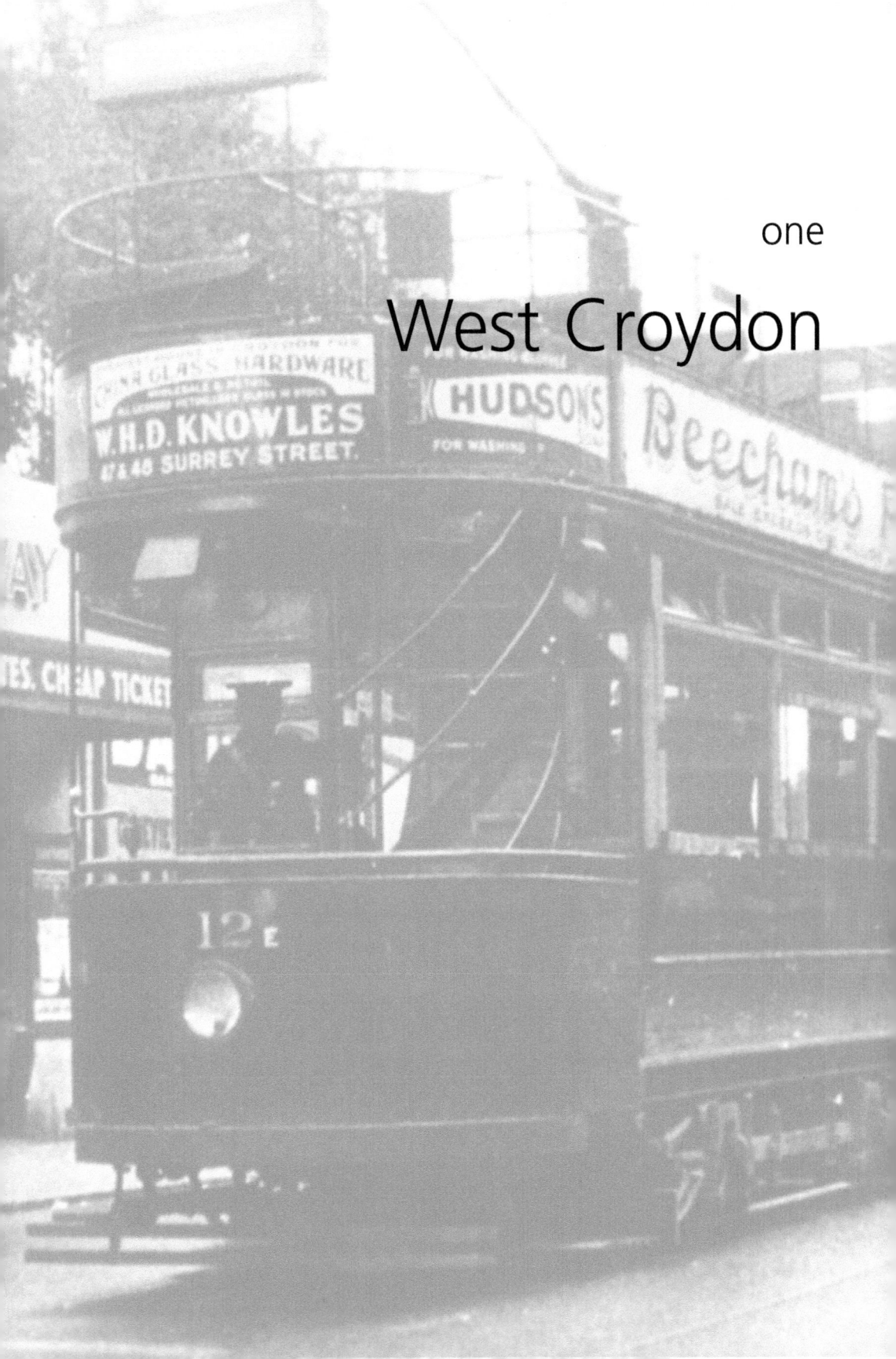

one

West Croydon

Above: London Road in the 1890s. The upper storeys of the buildings still look familiar in 2008, although the horse-drawn traffic indicates the period of this photograph. On the left is the Fox & Hounds pub which dates back to 1800. In 1874 John Goodman kept the premises and provided hunting facilities with an entrance in Derby Road leading to stables. The present building dates from the 1890s. To the right can be seen the gated entrance to the courtyard outside the original West Croydon Station building.

Below: Two well-known retail names opened their first stores in Croydon in London Road. Marks & Spencer opened their penny bazaar in 1906 next door to Sainsbury's, who had established their grocery shop in 1900. Marks & Spencer moved to their present North End site in 1925.

London Road, West Croydon, taken from the courtyard of the original West Croydon Station. The first railway line to Croydon was the London & Croydon Railway, opened on 5 June 1839 on the route of the Croydon Canal. Station House, the building on the right, was all that remained of the very first group of station offices erected in 1839. In 1933 the old Station House disappeared in the West Croydon Station modernisation scheme, although the courtyard still survives as a car park. Through the station-yard gates can be seen Sainsbury's.

The 4th Queen's Royal Regiment was Croydon's territorial battalion. Its origins were in the 1850s as the Croydon Rifle Volunteer Co. On 5 August 1914 the Territorials, having marched from Mitcham Road Barracks, are seen here on London Road, passing Oakfield Road on their way to East Croydon Station, where the soldiers were to travel to Strood for embarkation.

Left: The first Wesleyan Methodist congregation established themselves at a chapel in Tamworth Road in 1858 but moved in 1900 to a new church built in London Road. Due to dwindling attendance, the church was demolished in 1957 and the present, much smaller church, opened in 1960, lies behind the site of the original building.

Below: Croydon General Hospital was founded in 1867 by public subscription with fourteen beds in the Croydon Union Infirmary at Duppas Hill. It then moved and opened at Oakfield Lodge in London Road, West Croydon, on 27 September 1873. A contemporary advertisement for the hospital stated it was 'For the benefit of persons engaged in the Industrial Occupations of Life (including Domestic Servants).'

Right: Extensions to the hospital were constructed in 1927, incorporating a new outpatients department, casualty and pathological block, which were formally opened on 25 June 1927 by King George V and Queen Mary. Royal trumpeters blew a fanfare on the arrival of the King and Queen.

Below: On the day of the Royal visit little Alfred Drew of Beddington is being cared for by one of the nurses in the Princess Mary cot, a wedding present from the townspeople of Croydon to Princess Mary on her marriage to Henry Lascelles in 1922. Since the 1980s, facilities at Croydon General Hospital were gradually transferred to Mayday University Hospital. Final closure took place in 1996 and the original buildings have since been demolished.

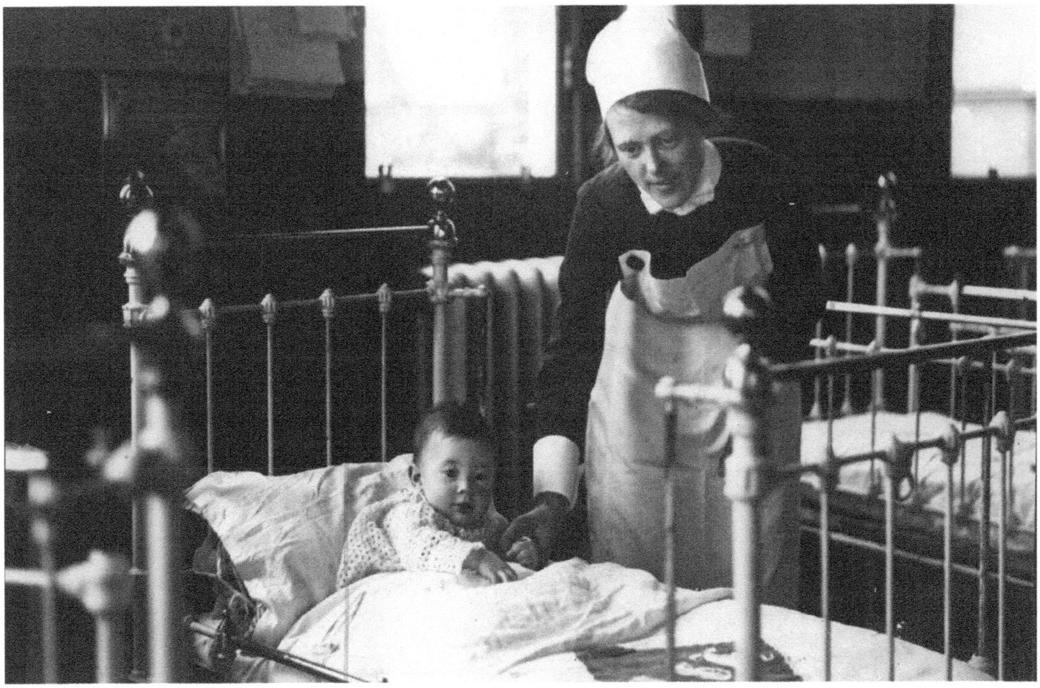

The original road bridge over the West Croydon to Epsom railway line in 1906. The block of shops in North End, still surviving today, were built on the site of North End House which in 1894 became the Gordon Boys' Home. To the left is Station Road.

The Railway Bell public house situated on the corner of North End and Tamworth Road. The pub was one of a number owned by the Croydon brewery firm of Nadler & Collyer. The Croydon Corporation tram on the left is travelling to Purley whilst the tram on the right, owned by the South Metropolitan Tramway & Lighting Co., is en route to Sutton.

Moore's 'Presto' Motor Works, situated in Tamworth Road, catered for the Edwardian motorist and motorcyclist, also providing motor vehicles for hire. The rear elevation of their office and other buildings in North End can be seen in the background. The motor works finally closed in the late 1950s.

Hobden's bakery cart is advertising bread made with wheaten brown flour known as 'Turog' flour and produced by a company based in Cardiff. Advertisements for the day extolled the health giving properties of Turog bread. F.J. Hobden began his bakery business in Tamworth road in 1909 but by 1913 opened a new shop in Church Street.

Home Defence procession leading out from Tamworth Road into London Road on 6 May 1939. Even before hostilities commenced in September in 1939 Britain had been placed on a war footing. This pageant had been organised by the local National Service Committee to attract more volunteers to take part in training for the nation's defence. The bus on the right of the photograph is attempting to set off on the long run to Guildford. The tram on route 42 is proceeding to Thornton Heath High Street.

The original station at West Croydon was completely rebuilt in the modernist style in 1933-34. A second entrance led onto Station Road as seen on the left with the Southern logo over the canopy. The South Metropolitan tramcar is about to depart for Crystal Palace. The station entrance closed after the Second World War. Station Road and St Michael's Road were built on land once owned by the Croydon Canal Co.

The junction of Station Road and St Michael's Road in 1906. The horse is drinking from one of the many cattle troughs provided by the Metropolitan Drinking Fountain & Cattle Trough Association around London. The association was originally founded by Samuel Gurney MP, a rich philanthropist, and Edward Wakefield, a barrister, in 1859. Their main use in London and the suburbs were for the vast numbers of hackney carriage horses as seen here. Under the main trough can be seen the trough for dogs and the boy is drinking from the water fountain provided for humans!

Railway Crescent in Station Road was the name given to the row of lock-up shops erected in 1907 on the site of a horticultural nursery. These were demolished to make way for the large office development completed in 1991 known as Prospect West.

St Michael's Church, on the corner of Poplar Walk and Station Road, is one of two churches within London Borough of Croydon designed by the celebrated architect, John Loughborough Pearson. St Michael's is considered to be one of his finest churches. His other church is St John's, Upper Norwood. The foundation stone of St Michael's was laid in 1880 and the consecration took place on 1 October 1883. The tower on the Poplar Walk side was never completed due to a shortage of funds. Erected in 1904, the adjacent vicarage in a neo-Wren style was designed by H.B. Walters, an architect and sacristan of the church. The vicarage was demolished in 1982.

Once private residences, the YWCA moved into Leamington Villas on the south side of Poplar Walk in 1905. By 1913 the YWCA had relocated to 87 London Road and these large Victorian houses were then occupied by the Territorial Army. The site is now the piazza next to Green Park House.

The Alhambra public house on the corner of Poplar Walk and Wellesley Road on 4 May 1960. Opened firstly as a beer house shortly before 1870 it became licensed premises a few years later. Both the pub and the other houses seen in the photograph were demolished to make way for the British Telecom building, Delta Point, dating from the 1980s, and Alhambra House.

In 1947 war damage is still evident to these three-storeyed houses in Wellesley Road. The trolleybus on route 654, which ran from Crystal Palace to Sutton, is about to swing round into Station Road. Just to the right of the trolleybus can be seen St Mary's Roman Catholic Church, designed in 1864 by Edward Pugin, son of the Gothic Revivalist architect, Augustus Pugin.

On 17 June 1869 three nuns of the Congregation of the Daughters of Mary and Joseph took up residence in Poplar Villa in Wellesley Road, Croydon, to found a school. Two years later the school moved to a larger property, Milton House, in Tavistock Road. The school was named Coloma after the Spanish Count of Santa Coloma, former owner of the Daughters of Mary and Joseph's Mother House in Malines in Belgium. Further property was acquired in Tavistock Road and by 1902 the main classroom block had been built. The kindergarten moved into separate houses purchased in Bedford Park, seen here on the right of the photograph. In July 1965, Coloma moved from Tavistock Road to the present site in Shirley Hills Road while Tavistock Gate now occupies the site of the old school.

Part of the development and extensions of Coloma Convent School was the chapel constructed in 1889 described in the March 1919 of the school magazine as 'no less beautiful; the harmony of colour, the simplicity and beauty of the Stations of the Cross, the Pieta, all combine to produce an effect at once impressive and devotional.'

West Croydon Baptist Church, or Spurgeon's Tabernacle as the church became known – named after its first minister, the Revd James Archer Spurgeon and brother of the famous Baptist preacher, the Revd Charles Haddon Spurgeon. Built in 1873 with seating for 1,100, it is a Grade II Listed building situated on the junction of St James's Road, Wellesley Road and Whitehorse Road. The adjacent railway bridge is also known as Spurgeon's Bridge.

Almost opposite Spurgeon's Tabernacle and standing on the corner of Oakfield Road, St George's Presbyterian Church opened in 1869. The church closed in 1939 as many of the congregation moved away from the area. Since 1948 it has been a masonic hall and the interior divided up into a number of meeting rooms.

The clock-making firm of Gillett & Bland, originally formed in 1844, became Gillett & Johnston in 1877 and set up a bell foundry in their Whitehorse Road premises. Gillett & Johnson became world famous during the first half of the twentieth century casting bells for churches and other buildings in Australia, Canada, United States amongst other countries as well as the United Kingdom. This 19-ton bell cast in 1926 for Riverside Church, New York was at the time the largest bell ever cast in England. The foundry closed in the 1950s but the company name lives on as a clock manufacturer.

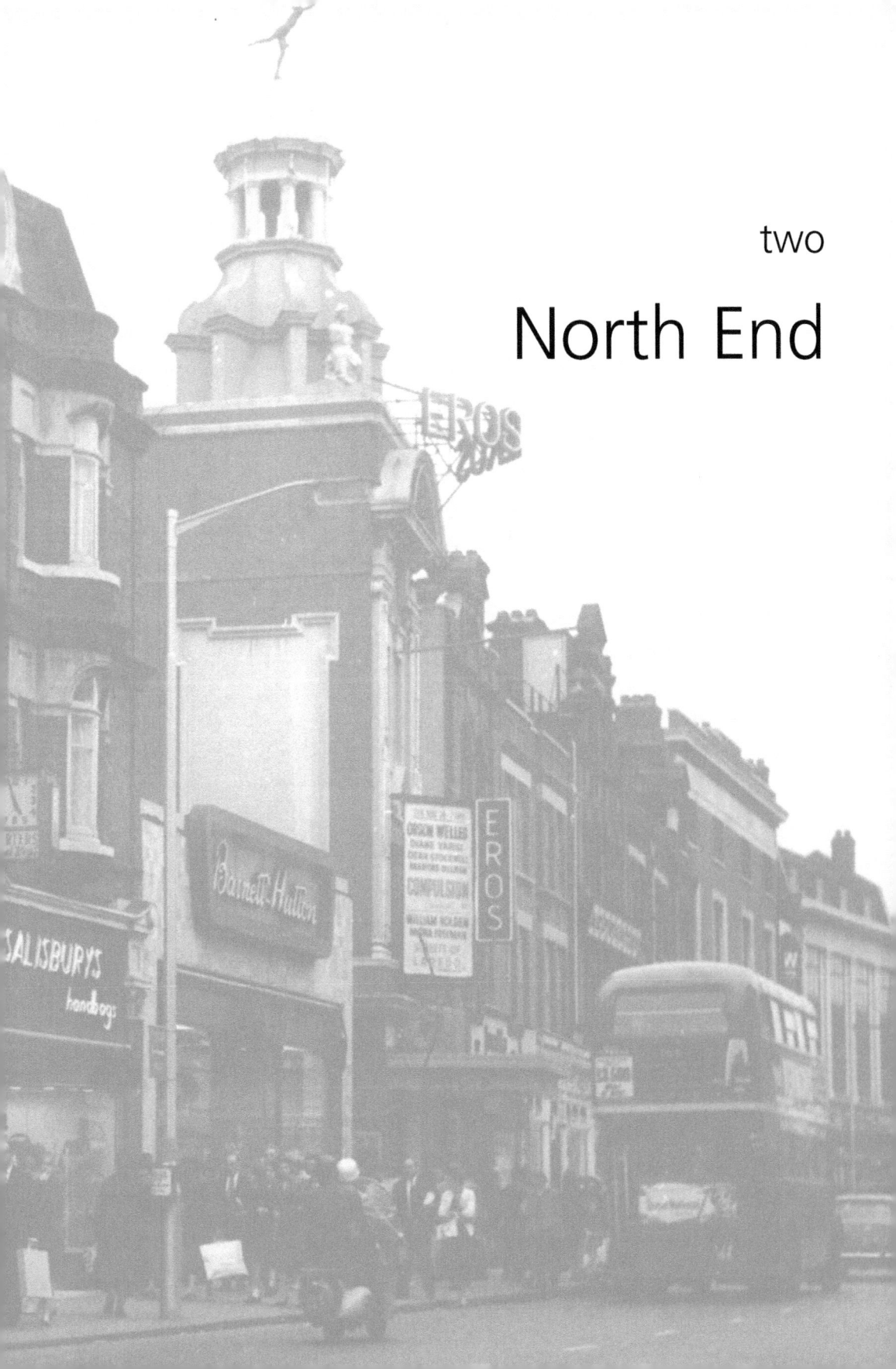

two

North End

Now a busy pedestrianised shopping thoroughfare it is hard to believe that North End was formerly a residential street which this photograph, dating from c. 1860, clearly illustrates although even in this view some commercial activity is taking place. In the distance on the left can be seen the inn sign of the Rising Sun public house, later rebuilt in 1906.

Compare this photograph taken thirty years later in about 1893. The lamp post on the right now by the entrance to Whitgift School is still there as well as the buildings on the right-hand side but many of the shops on the left are new. In the middle of the road can be seen a horse tram on the route from Thornton Heath. Bartlett's, the stationers, were well known in Croydon for many years.

North End around 1907 shortly after the reconstruction of the Rising Sun featuring half-timbered gables, balustrading, leaded bay windows and balconies. The building is now a Burger King fast-food restaurant. Next door is Stockwell & Oxford while to the left of the Rising Sun the shop carries a sign on the roof advertising one of the first phonographs.

The Rawling family firm began in North End when Alfred Rawling opened his shop at 137B as a jeweller, watchmaker and optician and as such he was listed in trade directories in 1903. In 1921 the shop is listed as 'A.J. Rawling & Son' as an optician only, although street directories for 1927 list Rawling as 'watchmaker.' This branch had closed by 1937 as the head office by then was at No. 8 High Street. Of the five sons and daughter who were part of the family firm, Douglas Oldfield Rawling died in 2002 aged 102!

Shoppers are here looking at the window displays of Kennards, while behind the lady with her bicycle are a group of girls clearly amused by the photographer. In the background can be seen Wilson's café with its sign advertising India Tea.

The National Baby Week procession winding its way along North End past the entrance to Whitgift School on Wednesday 4 July 1917. Compare this scene with those on page 24 and it will be noted that North End has been widened with new shop premises constructed. The campaign slogan was: 'It is more dangerous to be a baby in Britain than to be a soldier.' The purpose of the campaign was, in part, to give women the education that the government thought they needed in order to be better mothers. The council ran competitions and awarded prizes to the communities which held the most effective Baby Week campaigns. Two hundred babies and toddlers were entertained by the mayor at the town hall the previous day.

The first branch of Woolworths was established in Croydon in 1912. The section of the store to the left, featuring Portland stone pilasters and pediment, was at one time the Croydon Cinematograph Theatre which opened in 1910. Under new management from 1915 it was renamed the Palladium but bought by Woolworths to extend their store in 1930.

The Café Royal at 80 North End was a popular restaurant owned by the Pazzi family from 1889 until 1955. Originally established by Carlo Genoni and Adolfo Pazzi, both of Swiss origin, there was a large banqueting hall at the rear where many club and society dinners were eaten, as typified by this group in 1930.

The Empire Theatre opened in 1906 as a reconstruction of the National Palace Theatre of Varieties. As the Eros cinema from 1953, it only lasted six years and closed on 30 May 1959 with the demolition of the building taking place soon after. The narrow entrance to the Eros is now the entrance to the Whitgift Shopping Centre by McDonald's.

W.H. Smith opened their book shop in Croydon in 1927. The shop premises in North End feature ten full-colour coats-of-arms connected with their earlier branches at seats of learning: Rugby, Harrow, Eton, Winchester, Wellington, Croydon, Oxford, Whitgift, Cambridge and Surrey. At the opening of Authors Week on 22 October 1949 organised by the Croydon Writers Circle, the writer, Noel Streatfeild, is here signing books. She is remembered for *Ballet Shoes*, one of fifty-eight stories she wrote for children.

The Jubilee of Croydon's Incorporation as a borough took place in June 1933 with great celebration seeing many of the principal streets in the town centre decorated for the occasion. Kennards, founded by William Kennard in 1852 and one of the three principal department stores of Croydon, advertises that 'For 79 Years Kennards has led the Commerce of the Town.' Beyond Kennards can be seen Batchelars, which was bought out by Kennards. The store became part of Debenhams in 1973 and redeveloped in 1980, becoming part of 'Drummond Place', now Centrale.

Kennards offered numerous attractions including a children's zoo, donkey rides through its arcade and hosted many events. The winners of a Baby Week competition had a moment of fame when on 19 May 1938 the stage stars Lupino Lane and Miss Teddy St Denis came to Kennards to present the prizes.

Above: Joshua Allder set up in business as a linen draper and silk mercer at 102 and 103 North End in 1862 when he was only twenty-four years old. He built up the business to become one of the major retailers in Croydon until his retirement in 1902. Extensions in 1894 meant the disappearance of the Swan Inn next to the Whitgift Hospital. After his death six years later the business was sold although the name has been retained to this day. Joshua Allder became a well-respected local figure and took a leading role in civic affairs. For a while he was chairman of the Croydon Tramway Co. and it is believed some members of the shop staff were appointed to inspect tickets on the trams.

North End in the 1930s. The canopy over the pavement on the right belonged to the Scala Cinema, opened on 22 December 1914 next to Allders. By 1918 the cinema was being run by the Gaiety Picture House (Southampton) Ltd. Advertising boasted: 'Luxurious seats with arms in every part of the house.' Allders reconstruction of 1926 incorporated the Scala and its entrance. Although the Scala was in an admirable position to attract passing custom, many of the films it showed had already being screened by the other Croydon cinemas. It closed on Sunday 2 March 1952 and the site completely incorporated by Allders. On the opposite side of North End was one of three cafés in Croydon owned by J. Lyons & Co., characterised by the white-painted shop fronts and gold lettering. This café stood on the corner of Hedgis Yard leading down to Kennards arcade.

Opposite below: With continual expansion over the decades Allders became not just the largest department store in Croydon but the largest department store in the United Kingdom. This scene dates from 1984, showing North End just prior to pedestrianisation. The present façade of Allders dates from 1926. The 190 bus route no longer operates.

The aroma of roasting coffee from Wilson's Tea Rooms is one that brings back memories to many older inhabitants of Croydon. William E. Wilson opened a 'Tea Warehouse' in North End in 1883 and by 1895 added an 'Oriental Café'. Branches were opened in Purley, Bromley and Sutton. Wilson's moved from North End to George Street in 1960 when the building was demolished for road widening. They ceased trading in the 1970s. A large group of workmen outside Wilson's in 1926 are replacing the tram tracks in preparation for through running by larger London County Council and Croydon Corporation trams, shortly to be introduced on the 16/18 route from Embankment in London to Purley.

Aerial view of the Whitgift School in the 1920s. The name Whitgift remains synonymous with Croydon. Archbishop John Whitgift, who knew Croydon well during his visits to the palace next to the parish church, established not only a hospital on the corner of North End and George Street but also a schoolhouse and schoolmaster's house in George Street. The school accommodated up to eighty boys and was designated a grammar school, which meant pupils learnt Latin and Greek with the intention they could enter Oxford or Cambridge and qualify as priests or lawyers or servants of the state.

Following a period of decline, a revival in the nineteenth century resulted in the construction of a newer and larger building designed by Sir Arthur William Blomfield for 300 pupils on a site purchased between North End and Wellesley Road. This opened as Whitgift School in May 1871 under the headmastership of Dr Robert Brodie. In 1931 the school moved to a new site constructed at Haling Park, South Croydon, and Whitgift Middle (later Trinity School) took over the North End building.

Left William Earle, the groundsman of Whitgift School at the beginning of the twentieth century, was known by the name of Stumps, and a well-known character in Croydon at the time. Here he is seen sitting on the horse-drawn roller. The building in the background is Wellesley House first recorded in 1859 and former residence of Jabez Spencer Balfour, Croydon's infamous first mayor.

Below: One of the most famous Old Whitgiftians was Arthur William Tedder who joined the RAF, rising to the rank of Air Marshall and eventually became Deputy Supreme Commander of Allied Forces in 1944 under General Eisenhower. After the Second World War, Tedder was created a baron. In this photograph, taken in 1906 outside the Junior School building constructed in 1897, he is third boy in the second row from the left, holding a trophy.

Opposite above: Junior School in 1929. By this time plans were in progress to relocate the Whitgift School to a new site purchased at Haling Park, South Croydon. The following year, on 31 May 1930, the foundation stone of the new building was laid.

Below: Mason's Junior cricketing XI 1929. In 1904 the headmaster, Samuel Andrew, established the 'house system', one of the first in a day school, under Cross, Dodd, Mason and Tate. The Revd MHH 'Pop' Mason was born the son of an artist in London on 5 October 1860. He came to Whitgift in 1887 during Dr Brodie's headmastership and stayed as a master for thirty-seven years. He was housemaster of 'Mason's' from its institution in 1904. Behind the team is the thatched sports pavilion.

Above: Samuel Ogden Andrew, here seen in front of a group of staff, was headmaster of Whitgift School from 1903-27. Born in 1868 at Lees, near Oldham, Lancashire, and educated at Manchester Grammar School and Oriel College, Oxford, he also studied psychology at the Universities of Berlin and Tübingen in Germany. Andrew was appointed headmaster in January 1903 aged thirty-five but resigned in 1927. He died on 10 April 1952.

Left: 22 March is the date taken to be Founders Day, commemorating the day in March 1596 when Archbishop Whitgift laid the two cornerstones of his hospital in North End. Here is the Founders Day parade leading out of the school gates into North End. Staff and boys then marched to Croydon Parish Church for the annual service of thanksgiving.

These sixteenth-century almshouses were built in 1596 at the medieval town crossroads by Archbishop John Whitgift to house his 'poor brothers and sisters' and retired servants from the palaces at Lambeth and Croydon. Flags, banners and bunting decorate the almshouses and lamp post on the morning of Monday 18 May 1896 in readiness for the visit of the Prince of Wales the following day to open the new town hall.

Whitgift's 'Hospital of the Holy Trinity' is still used for its original purpose as almshouses and the quadrangle is a haven of peace and quiet in the heart of the town centre. Members of the ladies water polo team from Holland are given a guided tour of the almshouses by Cllr J.O. Pelton on 10 September 1927. Pelton was a noted local historian of Croydon whose father had owned a grocery business in the High Street.

The Whitgift Foundation took the opportunity to maximise the asset of land in the centre of Croydon by constructing a new shopping mall and office blocks on the site of the, by now, Trinity School. The Whitgift Centre, as it became known, was one of the first to be built in the country. In the centre of the open piazza was a pub known as The Forum, approached by a moving walkway. However, by the 1990s the Whitgift Centre itself began to look dated and could not compete with newer undercover malls in neighbouring boroughs so a complete makeover took place with the demolition of the pub and complete roofing in of the entire complex.

three

George Street, Wellesley Road and Park Lane

No. 4 George Street, c. 1866 when it was occupied by George Cooper, a surgeon. This house stood to the right of the old headmaster's house of Whitgift School. Allders now occupies the site. George Street takes its name from the George Inn that once existed where the NatWest Bank is now situated on the corner with High Street. Previously the name had been Pound Street.

This photograph of George Street taken at 9 a.m. on the morning of Tuesday 19 May 1896 illustrates well the preparations for the visit later that day of HRH the Prince of Wales. The old Whitgift schoolhouse, which when built in 1600 accommodated up to eighty boys, can be seen in the photograph to the left of the shops. The schoolhouse was demolished in 1897 to allow for the widening of George Street.

Right: This is believed to be Croydon's very first telephone exchange, in 1887 accommodated in a room at 6 George Street. The first telephones in the Croydon area were connected to the systems run by the United Telephone Co. and the National Telephone Co. Note the wiring hanging from the wall indicating the very limited number of subscribers.

Below: A scene *c.* 1930 looking east along George Street with the almshouses on the left, with the 1897 widening apparent. Passengers are boarding a 'K' type bus on route 12A while an 'NS' vehicle is on the short 178 route which replaced the Croydon to Addiscome tram route that terminated at this point.

The Aerated Bread Co. Ltd was incorporated in 1862 as bakers, confectioners and light refreshment contractors. ABC, as it became known, is mostly remembered for its chain of self-service tea rooms of which the first opened in 1865. At its peak it operated 150 retail bakery shops and 250 tea rooms across the country and was second in terms of outlets to J. Lyons & Co. ABC bought the former Whitgift Café in George Street in 1914 and the premises have continued to be a restaurant ever since. It is now Bella Italia.

George Street Congregational Church, September 1959. Congregationalists had worshipped in George Street when they first built a chapel in 1765. The chapel was rebuilt in 1843 and again in 1877. However, the church closed in 1962 when it became too large and expensive for the declining congregation and the decision was made to rebuild in Addiscombe Grove. A branch of Abbey now occupies the George Street site.

Further along George Street looking towards the junction with Wellesley Road and the site of the original pound. The shops on the right-hand side of the road dated from the end of the nineteenth century. Boots the Chemists opened a branch here in 1907.

A print dating from 1830 illustrating the junction of George Street, Wellesley Road (then called New Lane) and Park Lane with Fairfield House School on the right on the corner with Park Lane. The school was run by Alfred Twentyman until 1875. It is now the site of Suffolk House.

The Public Halls, c. 1910. The Croydon Literary & Scientific Institution was formed in 1838 and built the Public Halls in 1860. Until the Second World War the halls were the venue for many cultural organisations, musical events and exhibitions. The building housed a library as well as the first home of the Croydon Art School. When the Institution was wound up in 1929 Croydon Council took over the running of the halls.

A billboard advertising office accommodation in Norfolk House and building cranes photographed on 23 April 1958 at the same corner as the view above. It heralds the momentous changes about to take place in Croydon, transforming the centre from a market town to the largest commercial centre in the South East outside London.

Despite traffic lights it was still necessary in 1956 to employ a policeman to direct traffic at the busy junction of Wellesley Road and George Street. Note the typical fashions of the 1950s, the ubiquitous shopping bag and the brown-paper parcels tied up with string which the little boy, wearing short trousers, is carrying, and the school beret worn by the girl on the left.

J. & T. Robinson's electrical goods shop on the corner of Wellesley Court Road, photographed on 25 April 1957. The shop frontage had been built around early nineteenth-century cottages in George Street, the last survivor of which is now the office of Shakespeare's Undertakers. The buildings in this photograph were demolished in 1958 when Norfolk House was erected. Somerfield's supermarket now occupies this site.

George Street looking east at 12.35 p.m. on a day in 1956 from an upper window of Stevenson & Rush Ltd. The building with the clock tower is John Thrift & Sons Ltd, grocery and provision merchants whose business was originally founded in Church Street in 1857. The warehouse was demolished in 1962 to permit access to Southern House from George Street. Road widening meant the disappearance of the shops on the right-hand side of George Street where Suffolk House now stands. The clock in Thrift's tower came from Croydon's second town hall when that was demolished in 1893.

The newly constructed St Matthew's Church in George Street in 1866 as seen from the field opposite. With the rapid commercial development in the 1960s and the movement of population away from the centre, it was decided to build a new St Matthew's within the Park Hill housing estate. Consequently old St Matthew's closed and was demolished in 1972.

The interior of St Matthew's Church. The church was an example of the work of the Victorian architect Sir Arthur William Blomfield. An extension to the chancel was completed in 1877.

A widened George Street looking west in 1964. When Essex House and Suffolk House were built in the early 1960s replacing the shops seen in the photograph on the top of page 45, the church provided an excellent contrast in architecture. The tall block in the background is St George's House, home to the UK headquarters of Nestlé. Built on the site of the church, St Matthew's House is the administrative offices of the Croydon area of Southwark Diocese.

Looking west along George Street from the bridge at East Croydon Station, 11 June 1957. On the left is the sign of the Railway Tavern public house originally dating from 1841. On the right-hand side can be seen the turning into Dingwall Road. None of the buildings in the photograph have survived the redevelopment of George Street in the 1960s. At the time of writing there are two competing development proposals for the whole of the site bordered by Dingwall Road, George Street and the railway known as Croydon Gateway.

Woodford House School in Dingwall Road was established in 1867 and numbered among its pupils Dame Peggy Ashcroft, the actress, who attended the school between 1915 and 1924. The school had its own Girl Guides Company seen wearing the large floppy hats introduced during the period of the First World War.

Bourne & Balmer Ltd coach station in Dingwall Road in 1955. The company was first recorded as removal contractors in 1924. From 1933 their new coach station provided the departure point for regular services to the south coast and for tours. The company was later acquired by A. Timpson & Sons Ltd of Catford, who themselves later became part of the National Travel organisation.

Fremlins Brothers Family Ale & Stout Stores at No. 54A Dingwall Road on the corner of Lansdowne Road. The gentleman on the right is probably William Guthrie, the manager.

Lansdowne Road runs from Wellesley Road across Dingwall Road then bears northwards to St James Road. The whole estate of large Victorian villas, including these in Lansdowne Road, by the corner of Bedford Place, was developed on land owned by Thomas Russell, then on the outskirts of Croydon and yet convenient to East Croydon Station. Many of the Victorian villas were demolished in the 1960s and 1970s to make way for new office block development and apartment blocks, but those on the left still survive although much altered.

Members of the Croydon Fencing Club outside in the grounds of Wellesley House. This large house, built in the eighteenth century, was once the home of Jabez Spencer Balfour, Croydon's infamous first mayor. Wellesley House later became the hostel for the Girls Friendly Society. The Wellesley Road multi-storey car park stands on the site of the house.

Another school that has since relocated to a larger site out of the town centre is Croydon High School for Girls. Originally opened in North End in September 1874 with eighty-eight pupils under the auspices of the Girls Public Day School Trust, the school proved popular requiring a move to a larger house at 36 Wellesley Road in 1880 by which time pupil numbers had increased to 230. Further buildings in Wellesley Road were acquired and a new block constructed as seen here in 1904.

The school orchestra rehearsing in the music room *c.* 1910. A plaque commemorating the first headmistress of the school, Dorinda Neligan, is situated on the north aisle wall of Croydon Parish Church. She retired in 1901.

The playground behind the new classroom block constructed c. 1904. Increasing land values in the centre of Croydon and the need to upgrade the school facilities necessitated the move to a new larger site in Selsdon in 1966.

The Croydon High School Cricket XI of 1952.

Sewing lesson in the domestic science room 1948. Although girls were taught the home-making subjects, chemistry was added to the school curriculum in 1885 at a time when it was almost unheard of for girls to be taught such subjects.

Croydon High School Speech Day 3 March 1954 in the Civic Hall in North End. On the occasion of the school's eightieth anniversary the prizes were presented by Sybil Campbell who made legal history as one of ten women admitted at Middle Temple in November 1922, when women were first called to the English Bar. From 1945 Sybil Campbell became the first woman to serve as a stipendiary magistrate in London, at Tower Bridge Magistrate's Court.

Local ARP wardens are parading in Dingwall Avenue at the junction with Wellesley Road in the 1940s. Dingwall Avenue was laid out in 1889 in the grounds of Dingwall House, named after the Dingwall family who resided there and who were prominent Quakers in Croydon. In the 1940s the road was still lined with residential properties.

A further view of the junction of Wellesley Road and George Street, taken about 1910 with the balloon seller standing outside the Wellington public house. Woolwich House was erected on this site in the 1930s. The photographer John Henry Chick occupied the large house next to the public halls from 1906 until his retirement in 1929. Chick photographed the Old Town area in 1934 prior to the redevelopments which took place in that year.

Park Lane, looking northward in September 1903. Between 18 and 25 September 1903 the Automobile Club of Great Britain and Ireland arranged a 'Thousand Mile Trial'. Participants started from Crystal Palace and drove to various resorts in the South East. Here is an entrant travelling on one of the south-coast runs. In the distance at the junction with George Street can be seen The Wellington public house. The tree on the left marks the entrance to Park Street.

The formal opening of Croydon Fire Station in Park Lane, seen here in 1907, took place with due ceremony on 19 December 1905 by the Lord Mayor of London, Sir William Treloar. Replacing the previous premises in Katharine Street, the fire station was situated on the corner of Park Street. It closed in 1961 and was subsequently demolished so Park Lane could be widened to make way for the underpass and the Nestlé building.

Above: A queue of cars and AEC 'RT' type buses in Park Lane on 13 March 1956. The 119 and 194 bus routes still run in 2007. Today, the 260ft-high twenty-three-storey tower of St George's House dominates the scene, replacing the small shops behind the vehicles, while the underpass now lies to the left. Note the twin advertisements on the 194 bus for Biro, then a relatively new invention.

Below: In 1940 a shot down Messerschmitt ME109 was displayed on the Fairfield car-park site as a fundraising effort. The Park Lane fire station can be seen in the background.

Blakes Cottages in Park Lane, *c.* 1960. These early nineteenth-century cottages were situated opposite the Town Hall Gardens (now Queen's Gardens) but demolished in 1961 to make way for the Fairfield Halls and the southern approach to the underpass.

St Anselm's, a fine Georgian house dating from 1708. When the Society of Friends (Quakers) moved their school from Islington to Park Lane in 1825 they added two wings, one each side. These were later demolished after removal of the school to Saffron Walden in 1879. The house later became known as St Anselm's and survived until 29 September 1940 when it was destroyed by a German land mine. It stood where the flyover now meets Park Lane by Taberner House.

The earliest reference to Quakers meeting in Croydon dates back to 1657. The first meeting house was built in 1721 on roughly the same site as the present building, constructed in 1957 in Park Lane. The Adult School Hall, which adjoins the meeting house, was a gift to the Society of Friends by Theodore Crosfield and was built in 1908 to the design of the architect William Curtis Green. The roof structure was typical of the architect's work of this period.

Excavations for a new road to be named College Road taking place on 5 November 1959. The first technical college in Croydon was situated in Scarbrook Road. Plans to build a new Croydon College on the Fairfield site were first drawn up in the 1930s but the Second World War intervened. Construction eventually commenced in 1956. Suffolk House is under construction behind St Matthew's Church.

The junction of Wellesley Road, Park Lane and George Street was completely transformed by the construction of the underpass commencing in 1962 at a cost of £630,000. This was the eastern section of the town-centre ring road planned by the council a couple of years previously to deal with the problem of increasing traffic flows. The author recalls on his way to school passing the construction site and the deafening noise of the pile-drivers hammering in the steel piles into the ground. The tall slab block on the right is the Nestlé building built in 1962 and formally known as St George's House after Nestlé's old headquarters in the city of London.

East Croydon Station c. 1910. The first station was opened in 1841 by the London & Brighton Railway and a station to the west for local trains named New Croydon. East Croydon Station was completely rebuilt in 1894 in the then London, Brighton & South Coast Railway 'house design.' The present-day glass and steel structure which replaced this opened in 1992. Over 40,000 people use this station each day – one of the busiest commuter stations in the country.

Douglas Earle Marsh was appointed locomotive superintendent of the London Brighton & South Coast Railway in 1905. One of his I4 Class of 4-4-2T No 33 steam locomotives painted in the livery of umber brown seen here at East Croydon Station around 1920. To the left of the locomotive can be seen the sign for Hall & Co.'s Victoria Wharf.

George T. Hall, the son of Joseph Hall, one of the three brothers who ran Hall & Co, founded his own coal-merchant business but was bought out by Hall & Co. in 1911 and run as a subsidiary company. A three-ton William Allchin steam lorry No 1158 belonging to George T. Hall Ltd is at the coal yard situated west of East Croydon Station in Lansdowne Road in about 1920.

At the railway bridge outside East Croydon Station George Street becomes Addiscombe Road. Seen here in the 1950s the shops and the bank disappeared when the road bridge was widened in 1964. The building by the lamp post was home to Kathleen Harding, a solicitor, who for ten years resisted efforts to persuade her to sell the Edwardian house so development could take place. The NLA tower and roundabout were built leaving Miss Harding's home stranded in the middle! The bus station is now on the site.

These Victorian villas, built in around 1860 between the East Croydon Station and Cherry Orchard Road, became first Clark's College in 1910 then from 1914 the main office of Paish, Tyler & Co., the developers of much of Shirley and Addiscombe around Shirley Park. The main Royal Mail sorting office, built in the 1960s, now occupies this site.

Wellesley House School at No 20 Addiscombe Road c. 1930. Typical of the many privately run schools existing in Croydon before the Second World War, Wellesley House School was first founded by Capt. R.M. Pope in Dingwall Avenue in 1924 but moved to larger premises on the corner of Addiscombe Road and Addiscombe Grove in 1927. In 1930 Capt. F.H. Jones then ran the school. However, the school seems to have closed by 1932 after the death of Capt. Jones as there is no further mention of the school in local street directories.

In 1915 Frederick George Creed, Canadian by birth, transferred his successful teleprinter business from Selsdon Road to the former roller-skating rink opened in 1909 situated in Cherry Orchard Road. Many women were employed by Creeds during the First World War to make up for labour shortages caused by men fighting in the armed forces.

Creeds new offices on the corner of Cherry Orchard Road and Addiscome Road in April 1964 shortly before the business closed. Knollys House is now on this site.

A new bridge linking Barclay Road and Fairfield Road was built and formally opened by the Mayor of Croydon, Alderman A.V. Dammarell, on 15 July 1957. Once the later road link was constructed between Chepstow Road and Addiscome Road traffic was now able to proceed to Croydon without having to negotiate congested George Street. Government funding cutbacks curtailed the original plan to build a wider bridge.

With land having been purchased from the Ecclesiastical Commissioners for £4,000 for the express purpose of providing a public space for the town, Park Hill Recreation Ground was formally opened on a cold, miserable 11 July 1888. Snow had fallen that day at nearby Norwood. Most recreation grounds were provided with bandstands and Park Hill was no exception.

Left: The Park Hill Water Tower was erected in 1867 to improve the water supply to the higher areas of Croydon including the Park Hill Estate which was being developed at the time. Within the brick tower was a wrought-iron tank. Following proposals to demolish it, the tower became a Grade II Listed building in 1970 although it was agreed the water tank and timber supports be removed.

Below: The house at Coombe Cliff was built in 1853 by John Horniman, the well-known tea merchant. His son, Frederick John Horniman, founder of the Horniman Museum at Forest Hill, added the conservatory to the house after his father's death. In 1930 Croydon Corporation purchased the house for a children's convalescent home. It is now an adult education centre. Having become neglected and following a public enquiry in 1974 to consider its fate, the conservatory was dismantled, stored for some years and eventually re-erected at the Horniman Museum in Forest Hill.

four

High Street

The High Street, c. 1893. The overhanging building on the right was formerly the Red Lion Inn. Later the premises became part of Hammond & Hussey, the ironmongers. In the distance can be seen the overhanging sign of the Greyhound, at one time Croydon's most famous coaching inn. Note the narrowness of the High Street at this period; just room enough for two horse-drawn vehicles. The buildings on the left were demolished two years later as part of the High Street improvement works.

This, Croydon's second town hall, was built in 1808 at a cost of £8,000. The money came from funds left over from the sale of the wastelands of the parish after the enclosure of the common lands in 1800. It was situated on the west side of the High Street opposite the present junction with Katharine Street and demolished in 1893, a year after this photograph was taken. Pelton's grocery shop can be seen on the right.

Right: The triangle formed by High Street, Crown Hill and Surrey Street was known as the market area, originally an open space but, as in many towns, rows of temporary stalls were gradually replaced by permanent structures. This was certainly the case by the seventeenth century from which period many of the buildings appear to date. By the 1890s the whole area had become extremely run down. Looking up Oak Alley which led from Surrey Street to Middle Row, note the jettied building on the right.

Below: Market Street looking towards Bell Hill. Austin Warner's shop stood on the northern corner of Streeters Hill. Warner combined the trades of wholesale and retail potato and fruit salesman with that of furniture remover and a cow-keeper, quite probably keeping the cow (or cows) either behind or in the shop.

Market Street looking towards King Street, c. 1890. The shop with the wooden canopy belonged to Anthony Cooper, tripe dresser, at No 2 Market Street. The deep shadow on the left is cast by the rear of the butter market which fronted on to the High Street. Behind that is one of the lodging houses owned by Charles 'Uncle' Day who by his death in 1892 controlled twenty of the twenty-eight lodging houses in the market area, many of which contained on average twenty-four inmates, many of them prostitutes.

Looking along Middle Row towards Market Street in 1890. Just beyond, the small crowd gathered to see the photographer can be seen the jettied building on the corner of Oak Alley. From the census returns of 1881 it is known that a community of Italians lived in the market area. Demolition of what had become an extremely run down 'red light district' began in June 1893. The remaining short section of Bell Hill still survives.

Surrey Street, c. 1890, near the junction with Middle Street. Most of these old shops and public houses were demolished as part of the 1890s improvement scheme. A one-time landlady of The Old Kings Head on the right was the maternal grandmother of John Ruskin, the celebrated Victorian writer. His aunt married George Richardson, a baker of Market Street, where John Ruskin would stay whenever his father was ill and a 'walk on Duppas Hill' was needed. Behind the Three Tuns on the left was a bowling green and, further on, the old jail built by public subscription in 1803.

Overtons Yard, 1939. Page & Overton was the third major brewery in Croydon whose premises were situated between Surrey Street, on the right-hand side of Overtons Yard, and Church Road. A brewery had existed in Surrey Street for many centuries and by 1797 was owned by Henry Overton. In 1892 Nathaniel Page became a partner. Although taken over by Charringtons the name was retained until closure in 1954. The lady on her doorstep at No. 3 Granary Cottages is probably Mrs Pantany. Next door is the banana warehouse belonging to J.G. Burns, whose delivery lorry can be seen in the yard. Besides his brewing interests Henry Overton established the first gasworks in Croydon before these cottages were erected.

Surrey Street Market in August 1929. The earliest records of a market in Croydon can be traced back to 1276 when Archbishop Kilwardby obtained a Royal Charter for a weekly market. It is likely that a market existed well before that time and the charter only formalised the arrangement. Until the 1840s, Surrey Street was known as Butcher Row and a terrace of buildings near the Crown Hill end still surviving today is known as The Shambles. The market in Surrey Street has been held daily since 1920 and is one of Croydon's best-known features, providing a link with Croydon's past.

A war-time display of fabrics at Grants. The Grant brothers originated from Devon and opened a drapery shop in the High Street in 1877 next to the Greyhound. They moved into part of the new buildings on the western side of the High Street in 1894 and their business later expanded to become one of the town's three large department stores. Grants, still a family business, sold out in the early 1980s and closed soon after. The main frontage along the High Street was skilfully retained while the site was redeveloped as an entertainment complex incorporating a Vue multiplex cinema, clubs and bars.

High Street in 1914. The High Street was the main shopping street in Croydon before North End began to develop from the 1870s and 1880s. Harry Hawkins was the licensed victualler who ran The Croydon pub on the corner of Katharine Street. The upstairs bar was known as 'Batty's Bar' after a former landlord named Batstone. The shops on the left-hand side of the road were erected in the late 1890s following the redevelopment of the Market area. All the buildings on the right-hand side of the road, including The Croydon, were demolished in 1962 to make way for the St George's Walk shopping precinct, which itself is due for redevelopment for the Park Place retail complex.

The short-lived Croydon Central Station in Katharine Street first opened in 1868 with a line branching off the main London to Brighton route just south of East Croydon station. The branch never paid so the station first closed in 1871, reopened again in 1886 and finally closed in 1890. The present Town Hall was built on the site but part of the retaining wall can still be seen in the Queen's Gardens.

Troopers of the Hampshire Yeomanry forming part of the guard of honour in Katharine Street awaiting the arrival of the Prince and Princess of Wales at 2 p.m. to open the newly built town hall on Tuesday 19 May 1896.

Croydon's third town hall was opened in 1896 by the Prince of Wales (later to become King Edward VII). To the design of Charles Henman, it is a large, grand structure reflecting the spirit of the age and Croydon's status as a County Borough. The council chamber is still used for its original purpose, but nearly all of the council departments are housed in nearby Taberner House constructed in 1964-67. The Braithwaite Hall, named after the vicar of Croydon, contained the reference library and information centre until the opening of the new Central Library in November 1993. Gillett & Johnson produced the clock and bells, a gift of Alderman Frederick Edridge, for the 176ft tower.

The Ceremony of Exchange of Flags between Croydon and Croydon, New South Wales, Australia, took place in the afternoon of 20 May 1908. The party on the balcony, overlooking the main entrance to the town hall, included the Mayor and Mayoress of Croydon, Sir Frederick and Mrs Edridge; the Lord Lieutenant of Surrey; Mr T.A. Coghlan, ISO Agent General for the New South Wales Colony; Thomas Henley, MP for Burwood, in which Croydon New South Wales was situated, and his daughter; the vicar of Croydon, Revd F. Bird; and Rt Hon Arnold Foster, MP for Croydon, Surrey..

In June 1933 celebrations took place to mark the fiftieth anniversary of the incorporation of Croydon as a borough. Illuminated arches were installed in Katharine Street, suitably lit up on the evening of 9 June. Earlier in the day Prince George, the Duke of Kent, came to Croydon to take part in the celebrations. The buildings in Park Lane were demolished in 1963. The arches were later reused during the town's decorations for the coronation of King George VI in 1937.

Houses on the western side of Fell Road on 10 September 1960. By this date a few of the properties were occupied by small businesses although most were vacant pending demolition prior to the building of new council offices fronting Fell Road and Mint Walk. Fell Road, constructed in 1883, was named after the Revd Richard Crampton Fell, who once lived in George Street.

Above: Mint Walk looking towards the High Street, 6 May 1904. Until the nineteenth century Mint Walk, or Rope Walk, was very much an irregular alleyway between these early dwellings at the High Street end, while the eastern section of Mint Walk was narrow and straight leading to Park Lane. The name Mint Walk was first recorded in 1620. In 1864 Sarah Johnson owned a rope-making business at 27 High Street. Documents dating from 1868 list a 'Rope House' facing along the eastern end occupied by Sarah Johnson and her son and would confirm that they used Rope Walk to ply their trade. This eastern section was widened in 1896 but no longer survives as the Queen's Gardens were laid out in front of Taberner House in 1982.

Below: High Street looking north, 1890. Croydon's second town hall can be seen with its clock tower and bell. The premises of W. Stevenson's Family Grocery and Provision Warehouse would soon disappear in the High Street improvements. Stevenson's were well known in the town and later occupied a shop on the corner of George Street and Park Lane under the business name of Stevenson & Rush.

Croydon was crowded on Wednesday 2 July 1908 for the first Lifeboat Day Carnival for ten years. Over 200 horses were involved in the two processions through the town which included the Southend and Eastbourne lifeboats. There were fancy-dress competitions, decorated motor cars and various horse-drawn and steam-hauled floats. This photograph shows part of the crowds following behind the procession at the top of Scarbrook Hill.

Originally opened in March 1914 as the Orpheum with seating for 680 people the cinema became the Palladium in May 1930 having re-opened with sound equipment installed. Ticket prices used to undercut the Davis Theatre almost directly opposite. However, during the early 1950s the cinema slowly degenerated. It closed on 25 August 1956 with the last films shown being *Charley Moon*, starring Max Bygraves, and *Double Cross*. The present office block, Surrey House, was built on the site a few months later.

Croydon's Central Swimming Baths in Scarbrook Road opened in 1866 consisting of an outdoor pool and a smaller covered bath. In 1910 publicity for baths stated that the outdoor pool was for 'gentlemen only' in the summer months. In 1965 a site in Barclay Road for a new central baths complex was reserved as the existing buildings were in need of considerable repair by this time. However, when the building was demolished in 1974, funding was not forthcoming for the construction of new baths.

Residents of Henry Smith's Almshouses in Scarbrook Road celebrating Coronation Day in 1911. Henry Smith was a wealthy London businessman who set up a charitable trust to help the poor of Surrey. These almshouses were built in 1896. The fifty-four residents of these almshouses and the other main charity, Elis David Almshouses in Church Street, transferred to a new building in Duppas Hall Terrace opened in 1974. Mann Close is now on the site of the Henry Smith Almshouses.

A charabanc outing is about to set off from the Sheldon Arms public house on the corner of Sheldon Street and Wandle Road. Most of the people are wearing a small flower but it is not known what this represented. The Sheldon Arms and the building next door were demolished for the construction of the Wandle Road multi-storey car park.

Another view of the High Street looking north taken at the top of Whitgift Street in 1926. Compare this scene with that on page 78. High Street has been widened on the western side. Dearlino's, watchmakers, jewellers and opticians would soon be replaced by the Davis Cinema two years later while Wilson's electrical-fittings showrooms were demolished for road widening in the early 1930s.

With 3,678 seats, the Davis Theatre opened in 1928 and took its name from the Davis family who built it. At the time the Davis was the largest cinema in England and the second largest in Europe. Although used primarily as a cinema, many famous artists appeared in stage shows and the performances by the Bolshoi Ballet in 1956 attracted massive queues for tickets stretching for over a mile to East Croydon Station. Decorations adorn the façade for the coronation of King George VI.

Opposite above: Designed by Robert Cromie, the Davis Theatre included a mezzanine with café and dance floor, a stage to handle opera, and a magnificent Compton theatre organ on which Alex Taylor played regularly. Unfortunately declining audiences for the cinema forced its closure on 23 May 1959 to be replaced by the office block, Davis House.

Opposite below: Wrencote is often considered as one of Croydon's most attractive buildings. Its present name dates from 1880 when Howard Nalder, one of the partners of Nalder & Collyer's brewery, lived there. There is no trace of a link with Sir Christopher Wren, but one of his pupils may have built the house in about 1715. By 1955 the house was in a dilapidated condition, as seen here, but through a successful campaign a government grant ensured restoration and approval of Nos 119-121 on its left to be built in keeping with the original style.

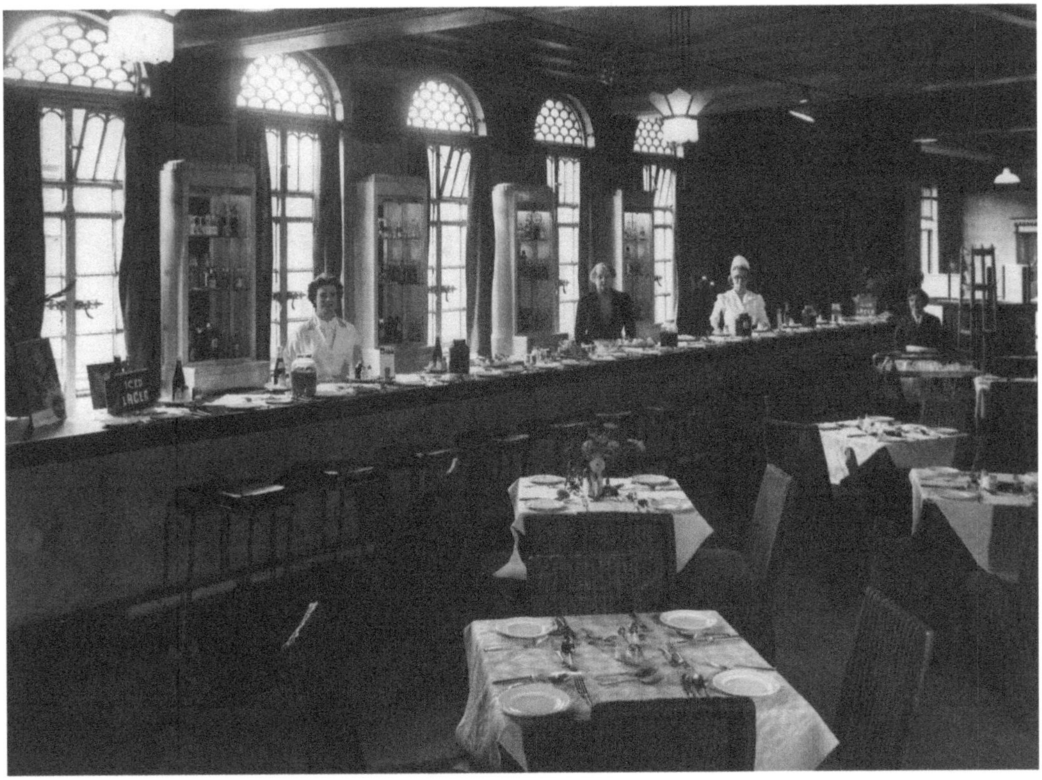

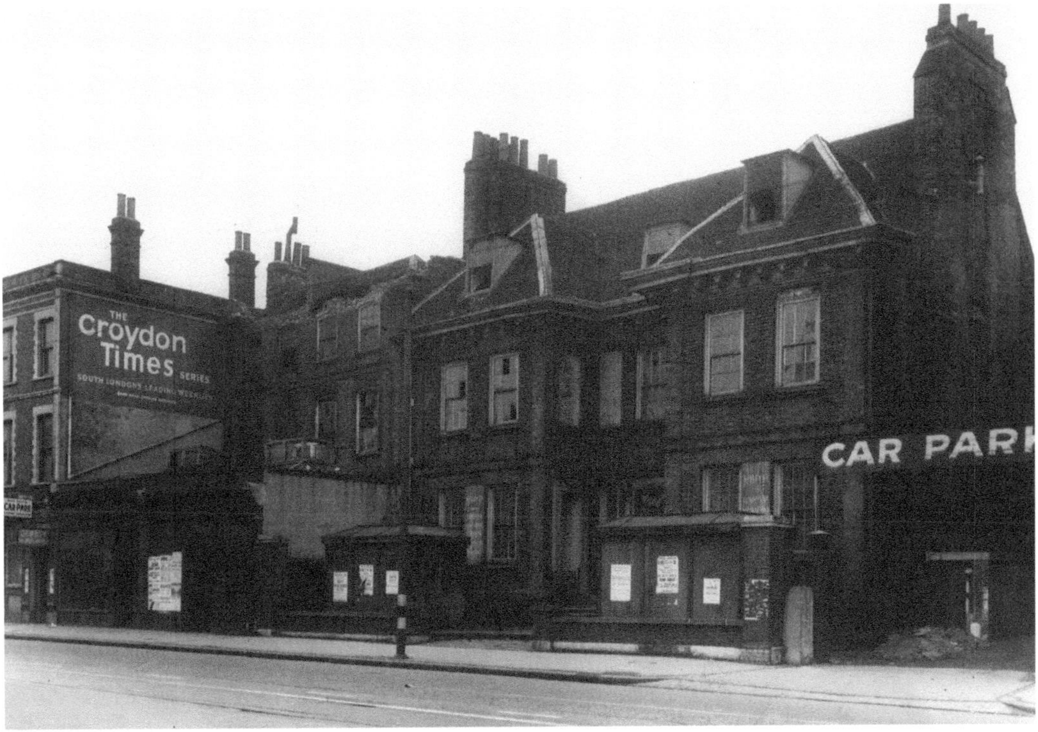
THE
Croydon
Times
SERIES
CAR PARK

Opened on 6 April 1896, the Grand Theatre and Opera House had a splendidly ornate late-Victorian exterior and interior and was a much-loved local venue. It had been built on the site of the Shrublands, the residence of Howard Nalder, one of the directors of the brewery next door. In the theatre's heyday, Herbert Beerbohm Tree (who opened the theatre), Henry Irving, Ellen Terry and Sarah Bernhardt acted there. Declining attendances forced its closure and demolition in 1959 despite local efforts to save the theatre. The site is now occupied by the office block, Grosvenor House.

Right: The ornate exterior was a prelude to the equally ornate interior vestibule and staircase. Nearly 100,000 people signed a petition to save the theatre but to no avail. The final show in April 1959 was *No Chance for Davies*, a futuristic spy story written by the last director of the Grand, Michael Wide.

Below: The music-hall entertainer and comedienne Nellie Wallace (real name Eleanor Jane Wallace) came to the Grand Theatre in September 1935, arriving in a Brougham to promote the next production, *Young England*. As can be seen behind the carriage, by the 1930s the Grand Theatre had lost its ornate frontage.

Brewing was always an important industry in Croydon. Behind these Georgian houses on the corner of High Street and Masons Avenue, photographed in 1964, can be seen the chimney and brewery premises of Croydon's most prosperous and successful brewery, Nalder & Collyer. A brewery had existed on this High Street site from at least 1586, which Francis Nalder, his son Howard, and Bristow Collyer took over in 1849. The brewery ceased trading in 1936 but the buildings remained in use for other purposes until demolition in 1964, when Leon House was built on the whole site.

Lower Coombe Street is on the left with the New Inn on the corner while Coombe Road, then Coombe Street, is on the right. The chimney of Crowley's Brewery can be seen in the centre with the dome of the Grand Theatre beyond. Flats now occupy the site of the Georgian building on the right.

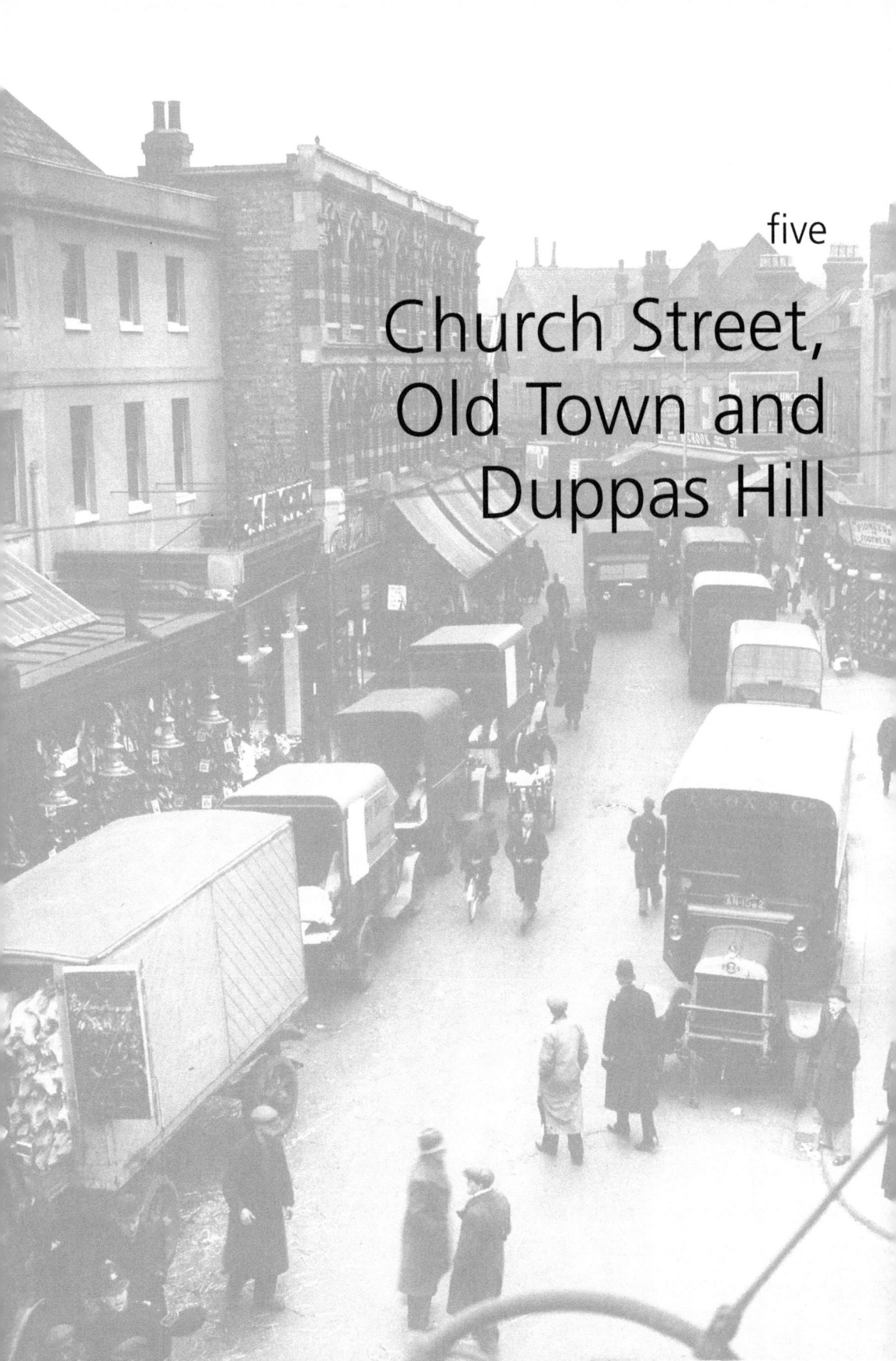

five

Church Street, Old Town and Duppas Hill

The Crown Inn on the right-hand side can be dated back to the fourteenth century but over the succeeding centuries has been rebuilt. The hostelry gave its name to Crown Hill, the upper section of Church Street opposite the Whitgift Hospital. Notice the sign attached to the public house advertising that telephone calls could be made there. The Crown Inn closed in 1940, but Burton's and Milletts established a 'Walk Round Store' in the premises until demolition took place in 1956. A branch of Barclays Bank now stands on the site.

Crown Hill in 1870 looking up the hill towards North End. On the left is the Theatre Royal built in 1867 on the site of a former theatre originally dating from the 1800s. The Revd D.W. Garrow wrote in 1818, 'Not many towns, perhaps in the country, have a theatre exceeding this in neatness and convenience.' The properties between the theatre and the top of the hill were still private residences at this time.

Right: The Theatre Royal was completely rebuilt and in 1910 opened as the Hippodrome showing films in addition to staging music-hall acts. By 1918 the Hippodrome went over entirely to films. In 1929 the cinema became the first picture house in the London area outside the West End to install the new Vitaphone system for talking pictures. Over 19,000 people came to the cinema in the first week. In 1931 ABC took over the Hippodrome, followed by the Odeon circuit in 1942 but the last film was shown on 3 November 1956. Note the sandwich board man advertising Burton's suits at 55s.

Below: HRH Princess Alice, Duchess of Gloucester, is seen here walking down Crown Hill on 19 January 1943 to formally open the Britannia Club, a club for servicewomen based in the former Britannia public house on the corner of Bell Hill and Surrey Street. Accompanying Princess Alice is the Mayor of Croydon, Samuel Roden. Members of the WAAF, ATS and WRENS formed a Guard of Honour.

Croydon has long been important as a centre for the meat trade and in the 1930s there were several meat wholesalers in the Church Street and Frith Road area. In early February 1936 a strike of Smithfield porters took place and for the duration of the strike Croydon became the principal centre for meat distribution in the south of England. For several days lorries and vans descended on Church Street and sides of beef and carcases of lamb were piled on the pavements.

Opposite above: On 9 October 1956 a fire broke out in the packing department of Kennards furniture repository on the corner of Keeley Road and Drummond Road. Rather ironic, considering the incised lettering on the building; 'Youngs Fireproof Depository 1864'! The fire engine attending the scene is a 1939 Leyland SFKT2 Cub Pump Escape based at the Park Lane Fire Station.

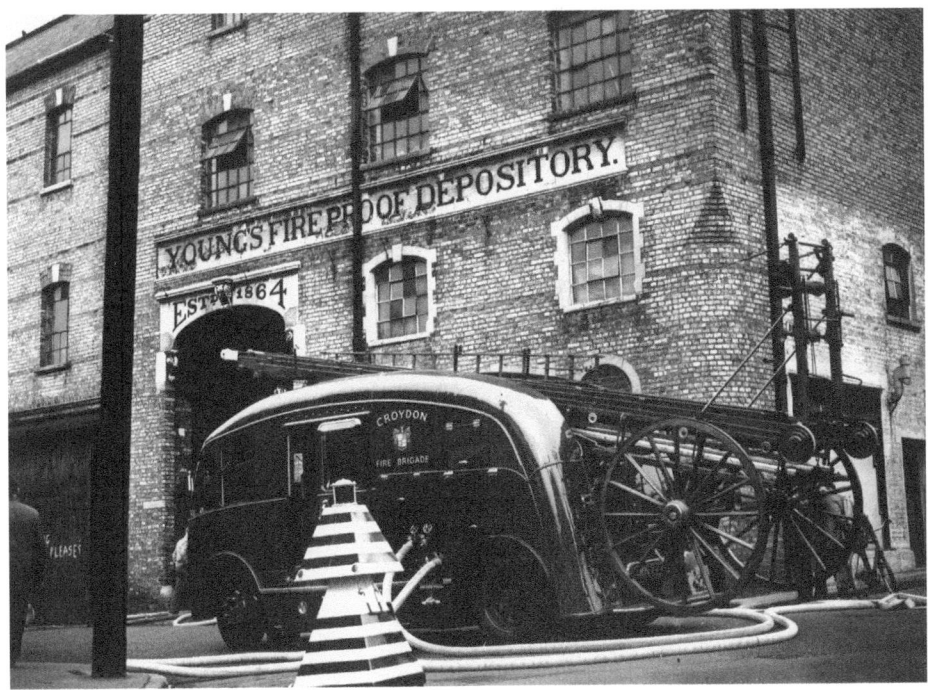

Below: Lower Church Street was the continuation of Church Street from Reeves Corner to the Pitlake Bridge over the West Croydon to Sutton railway line. In this 1950s scene a trolleybus on route 630 from Willesden has just come over the bridge into Lower Church Street before swinging round into Tamworth Road by the Spread Eagle to make its way to the route's terminus at West Croydon. This is now the position of Reeves Corner Tramlink stop, while New Life Christian Centre occupies the site of the shops.

Wandle Park, May 1913. One of the oldest public parks in Croydon built specifically for the purpose, Wandle Park was opened in 1890. It was created from poorly drained land, Stubbs Mead and Frog Mead, separated by the River Wandle, which was diverted to form a new course away from the artificial lake which became popular for boating at the turn of the twentieth century. Natural springs fed the lake, however in the 1930s the water table began to drop and eventually in 1967 the river was culverted and the by then empty lake filled in.

A further reminder of Croydon's meat trade were the buildings comprising the Croydon Abattoir, dating from the mid-nineteenth century, situated in the triangle of land bounded by Cornwall Road, Wandle Park and the railway line. These buildings were demolished in the 1980s.

The Shaftesbury Building in Elis David Road early on an April morning in 1961. This building was erected in 1867 and provided cheap accommodation but without basic amenities. The impracticability of bringing them up to modern standards meant the hostel was pulled down in 1961. The building with the onion dome on the right was formerly a market building built in 1906, a cinema from 1909-1916, and, finally, part of Reeves until 1973 when this area was completely subsumed by the Roman Way flyover and the slip roads which join it from Reeves Corner.

Edwin Reeves came up from Sherborne in Dorset in 1867 at the age of twenty-five to establish a barrel-making business, soon branching out into the ironmongery trade. With his sons entering in the business, Reeves eventually became famous in Croydon as furniture dealers and auctioneers. The Old Curiosity Shop at 120 Church Street, as the family business was first known, took over several neighbouring properties in Church Street, and now the House of Reeves, the company's new trading name, occupies most of the buildings on the crossroads of Church Street and Church Road. This area is now officially recognised as Reeves Corner. Edwin and his wife Sarah are standing outside the original shop.

Parish Church School infants class, 1933. The origins of Parish Church School probably originated as a Poor School for Girls supervised by the vicars of Croydon and held in the chapel of the Old Palace. By 1862 the Parish Church National School for Girls was in existence, which later merged with a new Boys' School and moved into new premises built in 1884 on the corner of Church Road and Old Palace Road. In 1966 the school relocated to new premises in Warrington Road.

A charter dating from AD 871 records that the Archbishop of Canterbury owned land at Croydon and the Manor is recorded in the Domesday Book as being in the possession of the archbishops. For centuries the archbishops used the palace as a country residence and entertained royalty on many occasions, Elizabeth I making frequent visits. By the mid-eighteenth century the location became unwholesome owing to pollution of the River Wandle and the trout streams surrounding the palace, so the building was sold, becoming a bleaching factory.

Old Palace Archway, c. 1880. This stood in what is now Old Palace Road just south of the point where it crosses Church Road. The arch formed part of the inner gateway to the palace but was demolished about 1884 when Parish Church School was built. In 1887 the derelict building was purchased by the Duke of Newcastle who donated it to the Sisters of the Church (a Church of England religious order) and since then the Old Palace has been used as a school and gradually restored and extended. It is now part of the Whitgift Foundation and is known as The Old Palace School of John Whitgift.

There has been a church on this site since AD 871. For several centuries the church and the Old Palace were situated beside the River Wandle and opposite the church was once Croydon Mill. The medieval church building was mostly destroyed by a disastrous fire on a snowy night in January 1867. It was rebuilt to the designs by Sir George Gilbert Scott, who used local historians' records and drawings to reconstruct it. Surviving the fire, the tower dates from the early fifteenth century. Archbishop John Whitgift is buried here.

In 1927 Croydon District Traders inaugurated the 'Streets of Adventure' carnival, so named after a popular book by Sir Philip Gibbs, to raise funds for Croydon General Hospital. Held annually on a summer Wednesday afternoon (early closing day) it became a great event in the life of Croydon. Here in 1937 part of the mile-long parade is moving along Church Street past the parish church on its way to Wandle Park. Up to the Second World War the total amount raised for the hospital was over £25,000 – a considerable sum then.

In 1858 the Governors of the Whitgift Foundation opened a Poor School in Church Road. Following a reorganisation of the education provided by the Foundation in 1881 this school reopened as 'Whitgift Middle School', a secondary school. In 1931 the school moved to the North End site and the Church Road buildings were demolished to make way for new council housing. Even in 1934 graffiti was in evidence!

Union Street, seen here in 1934, could only be reached by a narrow track from Old Town or a passageway from Church Road (see previous photo). The parish church tower can be seen in the distance. Salem Place and its council houses were built on the site, but not on the same alignment, shortly after this photograph was taken. Salem Place takes its name from the old Salem Chapel (see below).

Salem Chapel and Pump Pail January 1934. Pump Pail ran north east from the junction of Duppas Hill Road and Old Town to Church Road. The Housing Act of 1930 eased the compulsory purchase and clearance of the older and more dilapidated parts of Croydon, many of which were in the Old Town area. Salem Chapel on the left was erected here in 1729 for the Baptists of Pump Pail but taken over by the Congregationalists in 1866.

One of a number of photographs taken in January 1934 by John Chick illustrating the western side of Old Town. St Andrew's Mission Room and Infants School is the building behind the gas-lamp post with the alleyway leading to Prospect Place, one of a number of little courtyards and cottages hugging the hillside up to Duppas Hill Terrace behind. Next to the Mission Room can be seen Francis Woodham's grocers shop.

Old Town Stores c. 1930. The lady outside the shop at Nos 81-83 Old Town is Maud Curtis with her daughter, Eileen. When these buildings were cleared away as part of the 1934 compulsory-purchase scheme Mrs Curtis took over the shop at No. 25 Lower Coombe Street.

St Andrew's Church, on the junction of Lower Coombe Street and Southbridge Road, was consecrated in 1857 to serve the poor of this area, most of which either did not attend church at all or were chapel-goers. Within a year of opening, the church-wardens noted that the services, although full, did not attract the very poor for whom the church was built. The font has scenes painted by the artist, Cicely Mary Barker.

The origins of St Andrew's C of E High School began with the opening of a school in Southbridge Road in 1862 and a Ragged School opened in Old Town in August 1872 with John Jones as master. From 1908 this became St Andrew's Old Town School. Various reorganisations took place and in September 1930 the two schools came together under one headmaster in a rebuilt building on the corner of Church Road and Lower Coombe Street, seen here in April 1963. In 1964 the school moved to a new site in Warrington Road off Duppas Hill and in 2006 gained specialist music status.

Corner of Old Town and Duppas Hill Lane c. 1930. Note the sign indicating this was the main A232 leading to West Wickham. The shop belonging to W. Rowe, the fruiterer and florist, and the remaining properties along the right-hand side of Duppas Hill Lane were demolished to make way for the Old Town fire station in 1961. In the distance can be seen the Duppas Hill Hotel public house and Batchelar's furniture depository.

No. 19 Duppas Hill Lane, 1957. One of the last wooden houses, situated on the corner of Victoria Place, in the area to survive the Old Town redevelopment but was demolished to make way for the new flyover in 1967. From 1873 the property was occupied by Baldwin & Sons, builders and decorators.

The Waldrons, Croydon.

Above: The Waldrons was originally a private estate laid out in the 1850s with houses intended for the wealthy. This photograph shows the gated entrance leading into Duppas Hill Lane.
No. 23 The Waldrons was the home and studio of Cicely Mary Barker, the artist who created the paintings of the Flower Fairies.

Right: Cicely Mary Barker, seen here on the left with her mother and sister, Dorothy, was born in Croydon on 28 June 1895. In 1907 her family came to live at No. 17 The Waldrons moving to No. 23 in 1924. She became famous as the artist and creator of the Flower Fairy children's books. Cicely's artistic career began at an early age and in 1910 enrolled at the Croydon School of Art. Her work was commissioned by a number of churches including the seven sacraments which decorate the font of her own church, St Andrew's, and the Parable of the Great Supper for St George's, Waddon. Cicely Mary Barker died in Worthing Hospital in 1973.

Left: Waldronhyrst Hotel in the 1940s. The hotel opened in 1918 but closed in the 1960s. This advertising postcard was printed during the Second World War assuring potential guests that a deep underground air-raid shelter was available for their safety whilst staying at the hotel.

Below: Duppas Hill was the first recreation ground in Croydon on land purchased from the Ecclesiastical Commissioners by the Croydon Board of Health in 1865. Formerly part of common land of Haling Down, tradition has it that tournaments were held on the slopes of Duppas Hill until 1286, when Lord William de Warenne was treacherously slain by his enemies. The two men walking in the roadway would not be able to do so now as the Croydon flyover merges into Duppas Hill Road at this point.

Opposite above: Many of Croydon's festivals were held on Duppas Hill. Sir Frederick Edridge gave an annual firework display and bonfires were lit to celebrate local and national events including Queen Victoria's Diamond Jubilee. Field Marshall Earl Roberts is seen here on 9 July 1910 presenting new colours to the 4th Battalion of the Queen's Royal Regiment.

Below: A recruiting procession along Duppas Hill Road, 1939. Continuing the tradition of staging sporting events on Duppas Hill, baseball matches took place here between American and Canadian soldiers during the war years.

Construction of the Croydon flyover, the southern section of the Croydon ring road, commenced in 1967 linking Park Lane with Duppas Hill. Many of the small roads of the Old Town area were obliterated in the process with Church Road cut in two. Properties on the southern side of Duppas Hill Lane were demolished while Duppas Hill Lane itself became the northern slip road linking the flyover with Roman Way. Roman Way with Pitlake flyover became the western section of the ring road. Higgs & Hill were the main contractors. The official opening of the flyover took place in 1969.

six

Waddon

Waddon Lodge, a late eighteenth-century house, stood to the east of Waddon Ponds. During the early 1790s this was the home of Richard Smith, born in Cawthorne in Yorkshire, but who spent many years in Massachusetts and Connecticut in America as an iron master and merchant. At the time this photograph was taken, in 1880, Nathan Waterall, a retired timber merchant, was resident at Waddon Lodge. He is likely to be the gentleman standing next to the lady sitting on the wooden garden seat. Shortly after 1880 Waddon Lodge was completely rebuilt but when Nathan Waterall's daughter died in 1928 the estate, along with Waddon Court, was sold off to developers and new houses built in Waddon Court Road and Lodge Avenue.

Waddon House, an early eighteenth-century building, situated in Waddon Marsh Lane opposite to Waddon Lodge, photographed on 9 April 1901 shortly before demolition. At one time Waddon House was the residence of Philip Crowley, one of the partners of Crowley's Brewery of High Street, Croydon. In 1902, a gang of workman digging a sewer trench across the lawns of the demolished house discovered a series of caves, originally thought from the 'neolithic' period, but, with the discovery of another cave in 1953 in nearby Alton Road, now thought to date from 40 BC.

Right: Waddon Marsh Lane in 1889. Now Purley Way, the cottages seen in the distance on the edge of the lane still survive today on the same bend of Purley Way at the junction with Jennett Road. The name Jennet is believed to refer to the lady miller of Waddon, Jane (Jenny) Harding, who held land here in the seventeenth century.

Below: The centre of the old village of Waddon as seen in 1902 near the Hare & Hounds whose ornate balcony may just be made out in the middle distance.

Waddon Manor House or Court, so called since the manorial court met there, was a medieval moated site. Its site and adjacent grounds now form part of the public park known as Waddon Ponds, purchased by Croydon Council when the owners of Waddon Court and Waddon Lodge died in 1928. This long stretch of water is fed by springs and is now the only place in Croydon where the River Wandle can be seen. At the southern end the waters divided, curving round to form a moat in the centre of which stood the earliest manor house, now only a grass-covered area with trees. Beyond the water can be seen Waddon Court as rebuilt in the eighteenth century.

Waddon Mill can be dated back to the year 1202. Possibly of Saxon origin, some believe it may have been the mill mentioned in the Domesday Book entry for Croydon, although Waddon was not part of the See of Canterbury then. Documentation from 1448 refers to repairs to the mill. Over the succeeding centuries the mill was gradually enlarged and included two waterwheels and, by 1928, its year of closure, the mill was grinding 100 tons of wheat daily. A large mill pond existed on the north side of Mill Lane and survived the closure of the mill.

One of a series of photographs taken in 1904 of the farm workers at Waddon Court Farm.

Waddon Court Road c. 1928. On the left are some of the farm cottages belonging to Waddon Court Farm. In the distance at the bend in the road can be seen the rebuilt Waddon Lodge, while Alton Road leads off to the right. The late nineteenth century semi-detached houses on the corner of Alton Road were demolished when Purley Way was created.

A two-storey building with attic and cellar, the Hare & Hounds once had a fine ornamental iron balcony across the front. Livery stables stood to the south. In 1816 the Hare & Hounds was being used as a post office, served of course by mail coach. A further public house stood to the north called the Fox & Goose which was replaced by Victorian houses. The occasion and date featuring this stagecoach is unknown but is possibly around 1905.

Now Nos 335-345 Purley Way, the pair of semi-detached eighteenth-century houses on the right have low pitched roofs behind a parapet with two-storey side wings which once had fan tracery in the curved window heads. The present house numbers now indicate multi-occupancy, and single-storey shops have been built in the front gardens. The building on the immediate right covered with ivy is believed to date from 1686 and was once visited by the writers Charles Dickens and Wilkie Collins, and the artist Sir John Millais.

Waddon Station, c. 1910. The Croydon & Epsom Railway opened on 10 May 1847, soon becoming part of the London, Brighton & South Coast Railway. The original station at Waddon opened in February 1863 almost opposite the Waddon Hotel nearer Croydon than the present station building which was constructed in 1937 further along Epsom Road towards Purley Way.

Another view of the original Waddon Station about 1910. Most of the Waddon area remained as open country until the 1920s, as this photograph illustrates. Note the sheaves of corn on the field opposite the station. On the left is the tramway standard for the tram route from Croydon to Sutton.

Above: Stafford Road by the Waddon Hotel in 1911, showing how rural Waddon was well into the twentieth century.

Below: Stafford Road, *c.* 1930. Twenty years separate this photograph from the preceding view yet the parade of shops, known as Stafford Parade, had only just been built in 1928. Before the advent of supermarkets local parades of shops met the daily needs of most households and Stafford Parade in Waddon was no exception with its dairy, grocer, chemist, butcher, café and two banks.

The railway line near Waddon Marsh in September 1929 just to the north of Purley Way Bridge. The West Croydon to Wimbledon line opened in 1855 along the line of the Surrey Iron Railway, which had opened in 1803 from Wandsworth to Croydon, and later extended to Merstham in 1805. This plate-way line was for freight only, with horses pulling wagons. The London, Brighton & South Coast Railway electrified the line in July 1930 but it still retained an atmosphere of a country branch right up to its closure in 1997 before incorporation into Tramlink. Waddon Marsh New Siding branches off left across the roadway to serve Waddon Mills.

Waddon Hospital opened on 6 June 1896 and was first known as the Borough Isolation Hospital. This was in the days before antibiotics when it was necessary to treat patients with infectious diseases by keeping them away from the main community. The hospital was renamed Waddon Hospital in 1943 and in 1970 an eye unit was opened there, by which time the need for the isolation of patients was no longer required. The hospital finally closed in March 1984.

An aerial view taken in 1929 shows the newly constructed Waddon estate. All the roads are named after Croydon Mayors and leading council officials at the time. Denning Avenue, named after Frank Denning, traverses the view from centre left to top right. The road in the foreground is Purley Way. Construction of the council estate by Perry Brothers began in the mid-1920s.

A few houses on the estate were erected by the Church Army in Violet Lane in 1927. Unveiling a memorial tablet on No. 72 to Lt.-Col. Philip M. Glashier DSO, killed in action in 1918 during the First World War, is his brother, Capt. E. B. Glashier, seen on the right. On the left, Prebendary Wilson Carlile, head of the Church Army, pronounces the blessing.

The interior of St George's Church in Barrow Road, completed in 1932, whose simple sweeping roof lines are typical of the work of the architect William Curtis Green. With St George's, Waddon, he returned to the simplicity of his early period associated with The Good Shepherd, Frensham, in Surrey (1908). Other associations with Croydon include the Adult School Hall of the Society of Friends in Park Lane (1905) and Red Court at Park Hill (1911) and, much later, All Saints, Spring Park (1956).

Purley Way Swimming Pool opened on 27 July 1935 and could accommodate 1,200 people. The cost of construction was £15,600. The charges in 1935 were 1s for adults on Sundays, Thursdays and public holidays, and 6d on other days. Art Deco-inspired posters advertised the health benefits of Croydon's 'Ozone Bathing Pool.' It closed temporarily during the war but by 1973 the pool was in need of urgent repairs and closed in 1975. The site is now the Wyevale garden centre. After the closure of Purley Way Swimming Pool a new complex opened nearby in 1990 featuring a new pool known as the Water Palace. However, funding issues forced its closure in 1996

Opposite: The iconic diving boards symbolised Croydon in the 1930s.

Waddon Court Garage 1925. In 1924 Arthur McElroy and Stanley Bird bought land along the newly constructed Purley Way just to the east where Waddon House formerly stood and established Waddon Court Garage. A successful business was gradually built and in 1956 on the retirement of Stanley Bird a new partner, Gerald Goldsmith, joined the firm. However in 1972 due to failing health Arthur McElroy retired and the company went into voluntary liquidation. It was bought by Petrofina and converted into a self-service petrol station. It is now owned by Texaco. Behind the garage can be seen the houses in Alton Road.

The Propeller Inn was built at the Five Ways junction on the corner of Denning Avenue and Purley Way in 1936. Owned by the brewery, Barclay Perkins, the inn became a favourite 'haunt' for Royal Air Force pilots based at Croydon Airport during the Second World War. Derelict for some time, the Propeller was demolished in 2006 as part of a regeneration scheme along Purley Way to include new community and leisure facilities.

Heath Clark School, originally founded in Winterbourne Road in 1929, moved in 1954 to the building previously occupied by Waddon Senior Mixed School in Cooper Road. With falling pupil numbers Heath Clark eventually closed in 31 August 1984 and for a while the premises became an annexe to Croydon College. The remaning staff of Heath Clark School are seen here at the end of the summer term in 1983.

Harvest Festival at Waddon Junior School, 1950. Waddon Infant and Junior Schools were combined from 1934 until 1952 when nearby Duppas Infant and Junior School was reorganised as a junior school and Waddon Infant and Junior became a school for infants only.

Purley Way, 26 July 1960, at the junction of Croydon Road which leads off to the left towards Beddington. The first proposal for a bypass road was mooted as early as 1908 but nothing came of this. In June 1911 the Roads Committee put forward a proposal for a relief road from Thornton Heath to Purley via Thornton Road, Waddon Marsh Lane, Waddon Court Road and Coldharbour Lane. The First World War delayed the project but work finally commenced in 1919. The new Purley Way, officially opened in 1925, was built as a bypass for the centre of Croydon and also as an approach to the new terminal building for the airport. In 1932 the southern section became the first highway to have sodium street lighting which was soon extended in 1936 along the whole length of Purley Way and Thornton Road with lights suspended centrally over the road as seen here. In the middle distance can be seen the farm cottages in the lower photograph on page 109.

Opposite above: Croydon Aerodrome was established in December 1915 for use by the Royal Flying Corps as part of the air defence of London, using land of Manor Farm to the west of Plough Lane first known as Beddington Aerodrome. New Barn Farm, to the east of Plough Lane, was requisitioned for the testing airfield attached to the National Aircraft Factory No 1. This area became known as Waddon Aerodrome. On 29 March 1920 Croydon became the Customs Airport for London. Initially the old Royal Flying Corps buildings around Plough Lane were used as the terminal buildings. On the right can be seen the level crossing for aircraft in Plough Lane!

Opposite below: As air travel became more popular and civil aviation developed, the Air Ministry decided in 1925 that the airfields each side of Plough Lane should be combined. The central portion of Plough Lane was closed, the old buildings cleared away and brand new terminal buildings and a hotel built on the recently constructed Purley Way. The new airport opened in 1928.

Left: International airlines flying into Croydon included SABENA, KLM, Swissair, Aer Lingus, Air France and the German airline Lufthansa, who operated a fleet of Junkers Ju52/Ms. Here, D-ASIS is flying in to Croydon over the main terminal building in 1938.

Below: Probably the most famous types of aircraft flying from Croydon were the Handley Page HP42s operated by Imperial Airways to various parts of the former British Empire. Entering service in 1931 these aircraft, typified by G-AAXF 'Helena', set new standards of passenger comfort, furnishing and catering.

Above: A De Havilland DH Dragon G-ACYR belonging to Olley Air Services, the most famous charter company operating before the Second World War, founded by Capt. Gordon Percy Olley in 1934. In 1936 Gordon Olley assisted the Irish government in the setting up of Aer Lingus.

Below: In use as an RAF base during the Second World War and returned for civilian use by 1946, Croydon became too small to cope with the new larger passenger airliners. This is probably the last picture taken of Croydon Airport in full operation on 28 May 1958, two days before Transair Ltd transferred their aircraft and staff to the new Gatwick Airport. Croydon Airport finally closed on 30 September 1959. Today the Croydon Airport Society keeps alive the spirit of aviation at Croydon in the museum established in the 1980s in the former control tower and terminal buildings.

Above: Watermans Dyers & Cleaning Works, 1927. In 1866 George Waterman bought the business of dyers and cleaners from Bailey Brothers operating from No. 24 South End. In 1892 J.J. Bishop bought the business and transferred it to his son-in-law, Hugh McConnell, who came from Scotland and was already a skilled dyer. Hugh McConnell built up the business and opened a new cleaning works in Waddon on 1 January 1910; the first factory to be built on what was to become Purley Way. The company boasted its own artesian well, providing the firm with 12 million gallons of water per year. The factory was extended in 1928. On the death of Hugh McConnell in 1938 his two sons, James and Fred, took over management of the company and from 1946 onwards several branch receiving shops were opened around Croydon with Trojan vans operating the collection and delivery service. For financial reasons the factory was sold in 1954 and a new company set up, Watermans (Cleaners) Ltd with head office and works based at Hamsey Green equipped with up to date machinery. Fred McConnell died suddenly in 1959 so his son, Hugh, run the company with his mother and sister as co-directors. As the next generation of the family had not entered the industry, Hugh McConnell sold the business in 1989 thereby ending almost 100 years of McConnell involvement with Watermans. Hugh McConnell died suddenly in 2005. Incidentally, the author's wife is the niece of the late Hugh McConnell.

Opposite above: Adjacent to Waterman's was the Trojan factory. The company, formed by Leslie Hounsfield, first set up a car factory in Vicarage Road, Waddon, in 1914. In the early 1960s some 12,000 'bubblecars' were produced. For a few years the company also established links with the world of motor racing to produce the McLaren-Elva. However, the company's main base was the manufacture of commercial vehicles typified by this diesel van painted in Brooke Bond Tea colours.

Opposite below: Bowaters factory and offices, 606 Purley Way, June 1961. This splendid 'Art Deco' building dates from the late 1930s when it was built by the Acme Corrugated Paper & Box Co. Ltd, makers of 'Kraft', a corrugated cardboard packaging material. The company was bought out by Bowaters, the paper manufacturers, in 1944, who continued production of packaging material until the 1980s. The building is now owned by MSL (Mechanical Services Ltd).

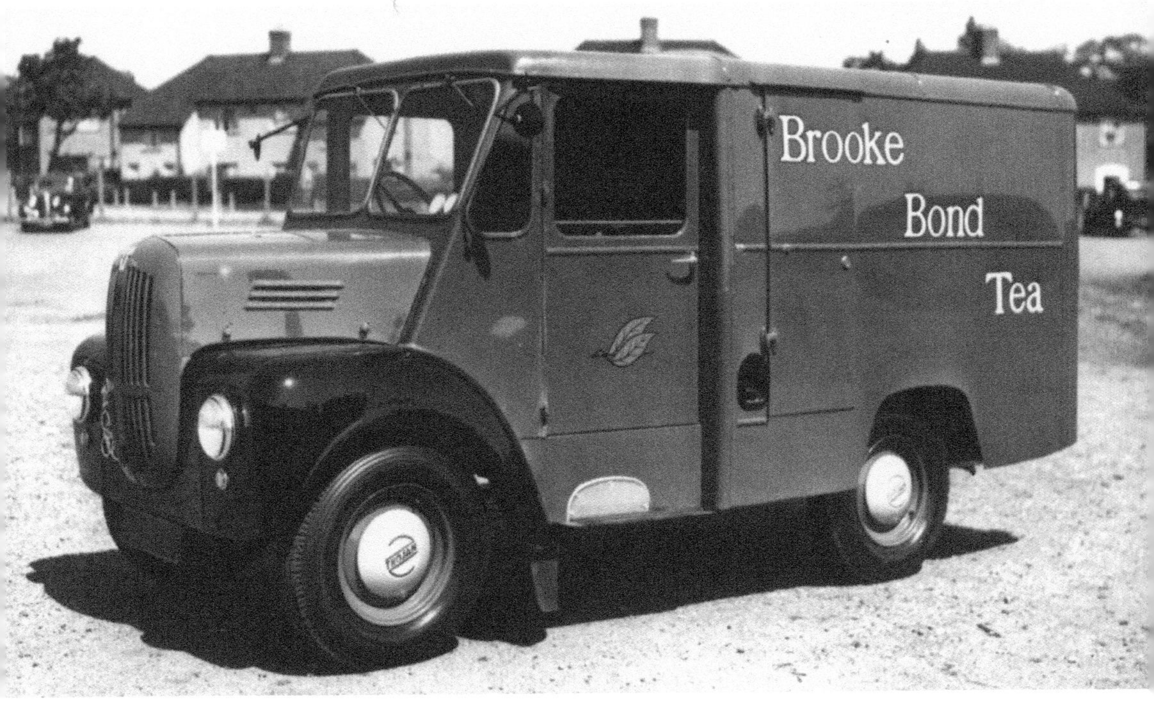
Brooke
Bond
Tea

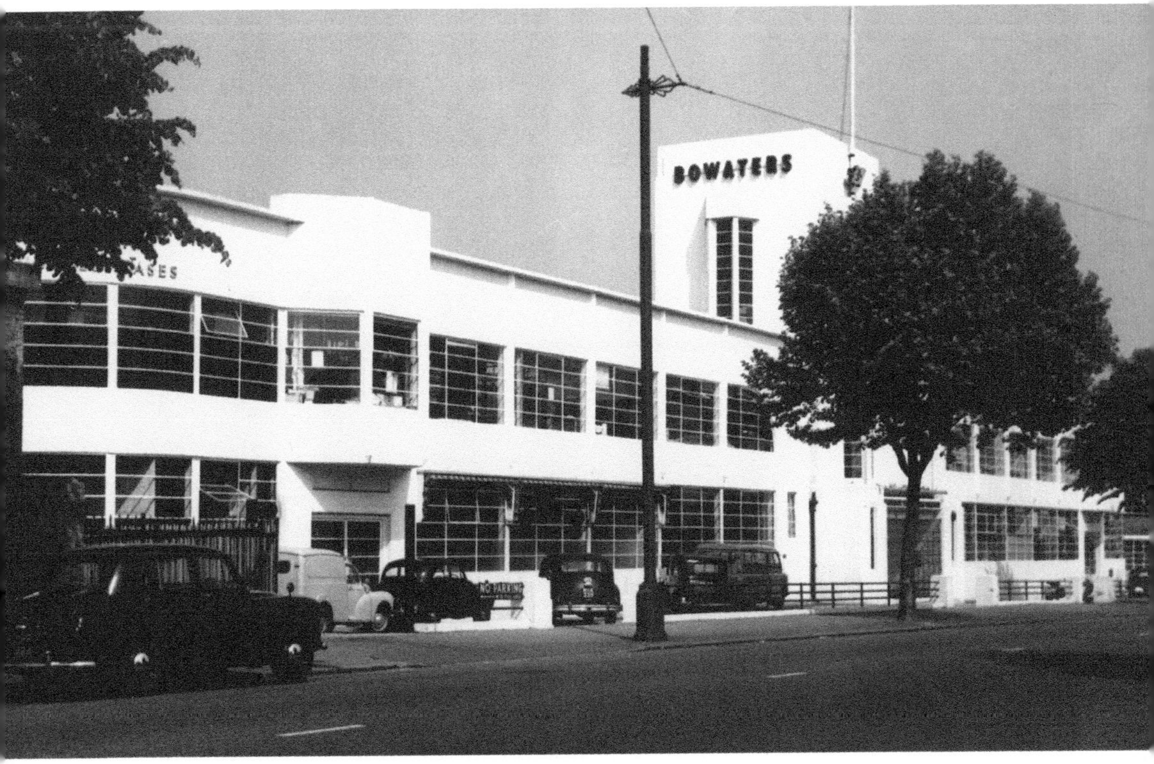
BOWATERS
NO PARKING

Purley Way, June 1961. With the construction of the 'new' road many industrial concerns sited their factories along Purley Way which become Croydon's principal industrial area. The National Aircraft Factory became Redwing Aircraft. Other light engineering firms were Louis Newmark, Walterisation, Trojan vehicles, Mullards, Powers Accounting & Tabulating Machines (Acc & Tab) which later became International Computers Ltd, Bailey Meters and Philips. Since the 1980s with the decline in manufacturing, warehouses and superstores such as Sainsbury's, Comet, PC World, and others have replaced the older factories. On the right is the Croydon Gas Works constructed here in Waddon in 1866 but only the gas holders survived after closure in 1976. The volume of road traffic during the evening rush-hour is in complete contrast to the traffic jams seen in Purley Way in 2007.

Virtually the whole area of Croydon and Waddon covered by this book can be seen in this aerial photograph taken on 3 June 1950 and is perhaps an appropriate one to bring this collection of photographs to a conclusion. The first Croydon electricity works with its single cooling tower, later known as Croydon 'A' power station, can be seen on the left in Factory Lane, situated opposite the gas works. The Kingsley council estate built in the late 1920s and early 1930s can be seen on the extreme left. In the foreground Croydon 'B' power station, first commissioned in 1947 and built by Croydon Corporation but soon nationalised under Clement Attlee's government, is under construction. The six newly constructed cooling towers stand next to Beddington Lane on the right and beyond them the filter beds of the Beddington Sewage Farm. The power station closed in 1983 and since then the whole area has been transformed by the building of IKEA, more retail warehouses, the VUE multiplex cinema complex, and new housing on the Waddon Hospital site seen here at the bottom right with roads given names inspired by power generation. The twin towers of the generating hall still survive as part of the IKEA retail store.

Other local titles published by The History Press

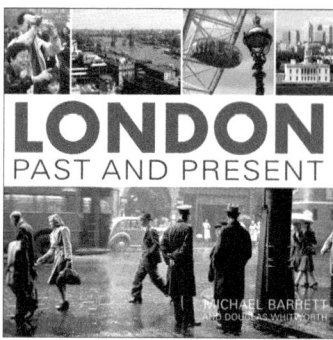

London Past and Present
MICHAEL BARRETT AND DOUGLS WHITWORTH

London has seen vast changes since the end of the Second World War. By using a selection of evocative images from *London in the Post-War Years* by Douglas Whitworth, Michael Barrett compares them with modern scenes taken from similar viewpoints. Featuring stunning colour photography also captures the daily lives of residents, workers and visitors, creating an important visual record of England's capital city.

978 0 7524 4304 1

Greenwich Centre of the World
DAVID RAMZAN

Greenwich has always been well-known for its position on the meridian line, however as David Ramzan illustrates in this new book, the area has a rich history with its commercial and industrial businesses in the town or on the river, and its naval and military connections. Illustrated with over 200 images, the book brings to life bygone days when Greenwich was a major tourist attraction. Although today much of Greenwich's heritage has been lost, this book shows what a wonderful place it was and still is today.

978 0 7524 4260 0

About Willesden and Wembley
LEN SNOW

In this anthology the history of the area is revealed through a series of articles originally written by Len Snow for the *Wembley Observer*. It looks at the makers of Willesden and Wembley, before going on to recall old Brent and the past way of life. Also included are articles covering institutions such as schools and hospitals, and personalities such as businessmen and sporting heroes. Evocative pictures from the Brent Local Archives add extra interest to the stories, and provide an informative and entertaining record of life in Brent which will appeal to all who know the area.

978 07524 4297 6

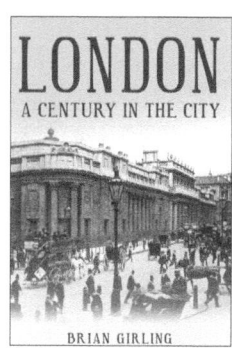

London A Century in the City
BRIAN GIRLING

Utilising rare and unseen photographs including haunting images form the mid-nineteenth century, the book offers an exploration and celebration of the City of London through a century from the 1850s to the 1960s. We may mourn the passing of that which was familiar to us, but perhaps this book will revive a half-forgotten memory or reveal times we never knew in a city which is known and loved worldwide.

978 07524 4507 6

If you are interested in purchasing other books published by The History Press, or in case you have difficulty finding any of our books in your local bookshop, you can also place orders directly through our website:
www.thehistorypress.co.uk